PRESCRIPTION IMPOSSIBLE

MIKE RICHARDS

Xulon PRESS

To: JESSIE

FROM: MICK

05. 04. 2015

DEDICATION

To my wife Joan, my children Peter, Paul, Ann,
Rose and Megan, and their families, and all those
who have faithfully prayed for us over the years.

CONTENTS

Part I Mahasarakham 1 9

Chapter 1
   The Mahasarakham Prescription................11

Chapter 2
   Frustrations 13

Chapter 3
   Developing a Working Formula................43

Chapter 4
   Progress and Shocks 65

Part II
   Pioneering an Evangelical Christian Student
   Fellowship..99

Chapter 5
   Initial Preparation....................................101

Chapter 6
   A Test Prescription...................................109

Chapter 7
   Opposition..123

Chapter 8
   Encouragements.......................................137

Chapter 9
   Tragedy and Growth 157

Part III Mahasarakham 2.......................................175

Chapter 10
   Travelling in Isarn 177

Chapter 11
   Christian Fellowship 207

Chapter 12
   Consolidation 219

Chapter 13
   The Final Product 249

Chapter 14
   A Pleasant Aftertaste................................259

PART I

MAHASARAKHAM 1

CHAPTER 1

THE MAHASARAKHAM PRESCRIPTION

Dr. Pavich Tongroach. President,
Mahasarakham University,
Mahasarakham 44150.
Thailand.
December 1996.

For The University Council,
Mahasarakham University,
Mahasarakham 44150.

Supply: One Functional Faculty of
                    Pharmacy of National Standard.
Instructions: To be used daily for the education
                    of students at Mahasarakham
                    University.

To be dispensed by Professor RME Richards as soon

as possible after he retires from his post in Aberdeen, Scotland.

Prescriber: Pavich Tongroach, PhD.

The above prescription was, on the face of it, a difficult but not an impossible one to dispense. However, after it had been written, the difficulty was multiplied many times to what many said was an impossible level, by the disastrous collapse of the economy of Thailand during 1997. My wife Joan, who is also a pharmacist, and I did not know the full consequences of this until we arrived in Thailand in January 1998. Nevertheless, I agreed, trusting in God's enabling, to explore ways to fulfil my original assignment.

What follows is an attempt to explain how that was done, in the setting of contemporary Thailand, but also referring to an earlier difficult prescription and some previous events and experiences in my missionary and academic career.

CHAPTER 2

FRUSTRATIONS

"We want to make sure you're not part of a scam" was the answer over the phone from the lady at the Thai Embassy, London, when I enquired why more documentation was required so that we could get our non-immigrant visas for Thailand. "But I've included the letter from the President of the university inviting me to take up the appointment." I replied. "You may have written that yourself. We need a letter from the President written directly to the Embassy." After several letters from the President to the Embassy officials we were eventually granted three month non-immigrant visas – not the 12 month ones we had applied for and expected.

This brush with Thai bureaucracy left us feeling aggrieved. After all had we not made a friendly offer to go to Mahasarakham, the second poorest of the 76 provinces of Thailand, to help establish a new university by agreeing to chair the 'Project to Establish the Faculty of Pharmacy'?

After arriving in Thailand a few months later, in January 1998, some of our Thai academic friends were also somewhat aggrieved and a lot of discussion was held on how best to extend our three month visas. The result of these discussions was that in March 1998, just before our three month visas expired, we arrived at the Immigration Department in Bangkok. We were driven at quite high speed, in the official car of one of the Deputy Prime Ministers and with his backing for a 12 month extension to the visas. My university contract however was only valid until 30 September and the official told us ever so politely that our visas could not be extended beyond that date! Our official driver remonstrated strongly on our behalf with a high ranking officer of the Immigration Department who appeared to be a police colonel. "The power is with the people," said the driver, "the people's representative has asked for 12 months extension and you must give it." "No!" said the officer, "the power is with the officials and they must follow the law." So we were each given a six month extension until the end of September 1998 and some kindly person (the minister? the colonel?) paid the 1000 Baht (£16) fee for each of our visas. We were assured that next time, as long as I had a one year contract beginning in October 1998, we would be able to apply for the full 12 month visa. In due course the time to apply for a visa extension again approached. We were advised by the relevant Mahasarakham university personnel to go to the

Immigration Department in Nongkhai on the Mekhong (river Khong) opposite Vientienne the capital of Laos. This was a much smaller set up than the Bangkok Immigration Department and actually a part of North East Thailand (Isarn). Thus although four hours car journey away it was a part of the same region of Thailand as Mahasarakham. For these reasons, it was argued, it was likely that we would be much more favourably received than in Bangkok. We arrived with all the relevant documents and full of hope that this time we were on the right track. It didn't take the rather junior official more than a minute or two to point out to us the error of the advice given us by the much more senior official in Bangkok. This was an example of the 'big small man' being as pompous and as unhelpful as possible. The argument now ran as follows. Since our original visas from London commenced their validity in January 1998 it was not possible to make an extension in October that exceeded a 12 month period from the validity of the first visa in January 1998. Thus it was of no avail that I now had a full 12 month university contract that could run in parallel with the visa since the visa could only be issued until the following January. Then in January 1999 we could apply for further visas, but of course these could only be valid for nine months because by that time I would only have nine months left on my university contract! The Nong Khai immigration official enjoyed this opportunity to demonstrate to us his authority and his understanding of immigration law and procedures. Another funny twist to the visa story occurred at a later date when the above procedure had been worked through. We were both applying for our second 12 month visa in Bangkok, in September 2001. The official who had been handed our application documents for final approval asked to see a copy of our marriage certificate, which of course we did not have. "Ah!" he said, "in which case your wife cannot have a non-immigrant visa". Fortunately the lady, who had previously checked through the many forms, official documents, letters and photocopies to see that our applications were in order before handing them over for approval, overheard what he had said. She came over and quietly told him that a marriage certificate was not necessary because Joan's bundle of documents, which he had not read thoroughly, contained her own contract with the university and her own work permit. That is Joan was not applying for a visa as accompanying me as my wife. So in fact all was perfectly in order and both of us were given 12 month visas.

This tendency of officials to seemingly invent obstacles at unexpected stages in the supposedly straight forward visa application process is certainly a source of aggravation to many foreigners. Particularly as it is essential to get it right in order to proceed to obtaining a work permit to take up a position of employment in Thailand. All foreigners must have a work contract, work permit and non-immigrant visa before commencing work. There are quite draconian laws available including prison, fortunately not often enforced, to punish those not complying fully with this legislation. The most likely thing that would happen to such a person would be that they would be required to leave the country at short notice. They could then legitimately return and start the whole process again. This in itself would be very disrupting, expensive and something to try and avoid if at all possible.

In my experience the procedure has been as follows. Firstly an appropriate work contract has to be supplied to the person intending to work in Thailand by the prospective employer. This has to be taken to the nearest Provincial employment office where an official notes that an application for a work permit has been commenced. The employer's work contract together with a note from the employment office is then taken to an immigration office (situated at an official point of entry to Thailand) where an application for the visa is made. If this is successful the newly issued visa is taken back to the employment office and an application for a work permit is made. This will run for the same period of time that the visa is valid. Work can then be commenced. Fees are payable for each visa and work permit extension. The cynical may see this as a possible reason for some of the twists and turns that occur in the process. On the other hand there are some foreigners with very dubious backgrounds seeking to take up residence in Thailand.

When in September 2000 we did finally obtain the 12 month visas from the Immigration Department in Bangkok (which we personally preferred), at our fifth visa application in total, we felt we had achieved the impossible and were thankful to God for having at last successfully completed the quite simple procedure. Celebrations were called for and we went to a nearby first class hotel, The Evergreen Laurel, and with great satisfaction enjoyed one of their marvellous buffet lunches. No mean enjoyment for those used to rural living. First class Thai hotel buffets consist of the best of many varieties of food - Chinese, Western and the different regions of Thailand - and are combined with excellent service that cannot be bettered anywhere.

Our going to Thailand, just after the economic crash, with the stated aim of helping establish a Faculty of Pharmacy obviously did not provide a very credible reason for our requesting non-immigrant visas. We were also soon to realise, on arriving in Thailand, that scams are not unusual occurrences in modern Thailand. Even people in high places are often accused by the media, or rivals, of being linked with such deceptions for personal benefit. In such a context it was unrealistic of us to think that we should be exempt such insinuations.

The rather exceptional invitation to me as a non Thai, to be the Chairman of The Project to Establish the Faculty of Pharmacy (The Prescription), was received from the President of Mahasarakham University (MSU), Dr. Pavich Tongroach, when we visited in December 1996. Pavich and I had known each other for many years. The possibility of my helping in some way at Mahasarakham had been discussed earlier in 1996 during an official visit by Dr. Pavich to The Robert Gordon University (RGU), Aberdeen. Then in December 1996 Joan and I visited MSU and several other universities throughout Thailand with faculties of pharmacy.

MSU was a new university and had only been established as a separate university for about two years. Previously it had been part of the Srinakarinwirot University, a university that had several campuses in different parts of the country. Thus MSU had inherited a campus and four faculties but it was now about to have a complete new campus developed five miles out of the provincial capital town with additional new faculties on a site that was previously indigenous forest/jungle. At the time of receiving Pavich's invitation we were prayerfully seeking God's guidance for what He would have us do when I retired from the position of Head of the School of Pharmacy at RGU. Our previous involvement with Thailand over many years meant that returning to Thailand was something that we were very open to. In addition I had previously helped start a School of Pharmacy in Africa and a Faculty of Pharmacy in Thailand and so I had some experience of what might be involved. It was hoped from the Thai side that we would be able to go to Mahasarakham at the beginning of the Thai universities' financial year in October 1997. But by June 1997 it was widely known that the economy in Thailand was experiencing severe difficulties and over the next few months, along with other countries in South East Asia, it suffered more than a 50 per cent drop in the value of its currency. Subsequently the faculty budget which had been agreed in principle for October 1997 was not now a possibility.

Nevertheless, after I retired from my position in Aberdeen at the end of December 1997 we believed that God was leading us to go to Mahasarakham. This we did in January 1998, with the encouragement of the President of the University, quite excited to have such an opportunity and challenge. However, we had been advised by Dr. Jinda Wongboonskul, a former PhD student at RGU and now a lecturer at the Faculty of Pharmacy, Khon Kaen University, that we would find general living standards very different from those in neighbouring provincial capital Khon Kaen. Jinda had made a special visit to Mahasarakham to check this out for herself and she was certainly right in her assessment. (She had also accompanied us on our first visit to Mahasarakham to see Dr. Pavich in December 1996).

Our Saturday midday arrival in Thailand coincided with the monthly MSU Council meeting in the parliament buildings, Bangkok. The Chairman of the University Council, Mr. Meechai Rojaporn, was also the speaker of the Thai Senate. Mr. Meechai had invited the council members and his panel of advisors to his home about 20 miles outside Bangkok for the evening and we were kindly invited too. After a quick shower at the OMF Home, where we were to stay the weekend, we were on our way with Dr. Pavich and Dr. Sangkhom, a Vice President of the University. On arrival we were given a personal tour of his gardens by Mr. Meechai in his golf buggy. Then we enjoyed an outside buffet meal and chatted with various Thai Diplomats who had served as Ambassadors in various countries. I was wearing a

Chulalongkorn University (the oldest Thai university) tie and this raised a query from one of them. He was a former student of Chula, and wondered how it was I was wearing such a tie. This gave me the opportunity to explain that many years previously (1965-1969) I had been a lecturer at that most famous of Thai Universities.

During the course of the evening we were told that the Project to Establish the Faculty of Pharmacy no longer officially existed as a university project as it had no funding and it would be necessary to find other means to support the development of the faculty. Possibly it could be connected in someway to The Walai Rukawej Botanical Research Institute, which was established as an autonomous research institute of the university. The position of Director of this Institute was vacant and maybe I could be made Director. Then in addition to holding that position it might also be possible in the course of time to have the Project for the Establishment of the Faculty of Pharmacy reinstated.

Arriving at Mahasarakham the following Monday was somewhat less auspicious than the special welcome we enjoyed for our Bangkok arrival! At the outset of our journey we were met at Don Muang airport, Bangkok, by Dr. Sangkhom and Ajarn (lecturer) Sunantha. They were to accompany us to Khon Kaen by air and then for the final 50 miles by road across some of NE Thailand's vast expanses of rice fields to Mahasarakham. Miss Sunantha was one of two lecturers who had been appointed in October 1997 to help establish the faculty of pharmacy. Her previous experience was at a senior level in a Thai government hospital. The other lecturer was Mr.Methin who had experience in both hospital and community pharmacy. Neither had previously worked in a Faculty of Pharmacy. Actually there was another lecturer, Mr.Woottipong, who had been recruited in December 1996, at the time of our first visit to Mahasarakham. He had been given a scholarship to study for a PhD at Mahidol University, Bangkok and so would not be available for several years.

While waiting to board our plane both Sangkhom and Sunantha were making somewhat worried phone calls on their mobile phones. In true Thai style we were not given any indication of what the problem might be. It became clear on arriving in Mahasarakham that the eight storey block of staff accommodation which we had seen under construction on the new university campus in December 1996 had not been completed. This was a little surprising because when I enquired about the accommodation in a phone call made to MSU in October 1997 I had been reassured that "tuk sing riabroi laew". That is, "everything is already in good order". My informant had been following the quite common Thai practice of telling me what I would be most happy to hear! In fact the economic collapse had meant that money was released more slowly for such government building projects and the building was months behind schedule. Just before our arrival somewhat hasty arrangements were made for us to be accommodated, at least temporarily, in a single room, plus shower room and squat toilet, of a private three storey block of student type accommodation in the centre of Mahasarakham. Sunantha had also been provided with a room in this same accommodation. Methin had his own house as he lived in Mahasarakham. Our room consisted of two single beds, an air-conditioner, hanging space for clothes, a shelf, a phone and a TV set loaned by the university. Having a second single bed in a single room meant that there was no room for chairs or a table and my case had to serve as a resting place for the phone. The only window was an internal one looking onto a communal corridor and we later found that this could be noisy even late at night.

Having seen the room we were taken to the old university campus about two miles away, where the Research Institute was located on about half of the third floor of the President's administration building. We were given a warm welcome by 20 plus staff who then wanted to know what their duties were going to be in future. This I could not tell them since I knew nothing of their current work. This discussion was left for another day. Both Joan and I were allocated a table and chair plus bookcase for me but little else. No computer, for example, although some of the other staff already had them.

Sunantha then accompanied us in what was now the early evening to what served as the local department store in the town centre. Mahasarakham was not very well developed and boasted very few of the amenities possessed by most of Thailand's provincial capitals. At the Serm Thai department store we bought stainless steel cutlery, Melaware plates, cups and saucers, an electric water heater, washing-up bowls and washing powder, towels, breakfast cereal, bread, marmalade, long-life milk (we had no refrigerator), coffee etc. Then we went to another place and bought a folding metal clothes stand and we were more or less set up for the time being. Sunantha then took us to the restaurant in a hostel for short term visitor's of a large College of Education which was on the edge of town. There were very few suitable restaurants in Mahasarakham and Sunantha, who had only recently moved to live there, was considerably puzzled as to where to take us to eat. After the meal and what had been a long and stressful day it was time to return to our accommodation and unpack a little. Most things had to stay in our cases. Then we got showered, had a time of earnest prayer and went to sleep. We had made it to Mahasarakham and the three days in Thailand had been full of surprises. Could we accomplish anything? Could we even survive? We were in God's hands. He had brought us here. Was that not enough?

Next day we needed to make arrangements for our daily transport, where to eat and how to get assistance with our clothes washing. We also set Methin the task of finding the location of the meeting place of a small group of Christians who had been recommended to us by the pastor of the Khon Kaen Chinese Church. Although Methin was a resident of Mahasarakham he had no idea of the existence of any Christian groups. Through persistence he eventually tracked the meeting place down. It was a rented house, with a large red cross at the front, about half a mile from the centre of town. This was a very important discovery for us and we met with this group of Christians on Sunday whenever we were present in Mahasarakham. The group consisted of about six or so adults, including Pastor Prasarn, and a variable number of children. Prasarn was supported by the American Nazarene Church which we did not know much about. The group that met in Mahasarakham consisted of two families and the Pastor's family actually lived in a district town about 20 miles away. The conduct of the service was very Isarn (the Thai name for the NE Region of Thailand) in nature – often using the Isarn language, which is more Lao than Thai, and thus not very easily under-stood by us. When we were present they would try and remember to speak Central Thai but this was not so easy for one or two of the older people. After the morning service they would spread mats on the hard floor and sit crossed legged to eat a meal together. The food was somewhat different from Central Thailand food, but we could enjoy most of it. The hard floor was more difficult. Our muscles and joints could not really cope and it was all too obvious that we were not comfortable, especially Joan, who had developed quite a lot of stiffness with the unaccus-tomed living conditions we were experiencing. Before many weeks had passed they provided a small table and Prasarn sat and ate with us. Later we all sat round a long table together. Our presence undoubtedly hastened the move to using a table but it would almost certainly have happened as others joined the 'church'. Having seen our living conditions Prasarn invited us to move into the house where the church met and even suggested that his wife could prepare our meals. We declined this kind offer because we still had hopes of more suitable university accommodation becoming available in the not too distant future.

The need for transport was temporarily solved by either Sunantha or Methin taking us to and from the old campus of MSU. A week or so later we had the use of an ancient pick-up truck, which belonged to the research institute, when it was not required for other things. This also was a fairly temporary arrangement but it gave us the chance to drive to Roi Et one Saturday. Roi Et (hundred & one) is a neighbouring provincial capital just over 20 miles away. While there we had a very tasty lunch at the Roi Et Thani Hotel. This was a great boost to our general outlook because eating out in Mahasarakham could not be recommended. Nevertheless, we had to do so for our midday and evening meals. The midday meal was mostly taken at the student canteen which had a variety of very cheap meals. We mostly chose a portion of rice plus a portion of a curry dish and a portion of a none-spicy dish to go with it. It was tasty but the canteen had very basic facilities and hygiene with many dogs and cats also sharing the leftover food on tables and plates. Some dogs rather aggressively demanded food from one's plate and could be somewhat intimidating – especially in a country where rabies is widespread. The evening meal was quite difficult because the choice was extremely limited and we often did not have transport. We mostly ate at a noodle shop round the corner from our accommodation where we received a friendly reception from the extremely hardworking cook. The food was tasty but the facilities were also very basic. We both enjoy Thai food very much but unfortunately many of the dishes local to the NE Thailand region were strange to us. A lot of sticky rice is eaten as the basic food. This is often rolled into a ball with the fingers, dipped into a spicy sauce or popped into the mouth with some raw vegetables, a piece of meat or fish. The fish could be hazardous because in country districts it is often eaten uncooked and could potentially transmit liver fluke to the eater. Once acquired it could be very difficult to eradicate. In NE Thailand, because it is much harder to produce a wide range of what we might consider typical fresh foods, some rather strange things are eaten and may even be considered to be a delicacy. Common items of food which were strange to us were rats, scorpions and various beetles but we have not knowingly eaten any of these items.

The hot dry climate and the poor soil are largely responsible for the restricted variety of food and the poverty of the people. Over the years there have been many attempts to improve the situation. These range from the traditional custom of building rockets and firing them high into the sky in an attempt to bring rain at the beginning of the rainy season to irrigation projects and the building of small and large dams. The latter have had mixed success, but I believe the situation is much better than 40 years ago and a large quantity of rice is produced. More than 20 million people live in NE Thailand making it Thailand's biggest region.

Our long term transport needs were generously solved by Dr. Pavich who forewent the provision of a personal car for his use in Bangkok so that we could use it in Mahasarakham. I have a lifelong Thai driving licence dating from the early 1960s and this meant I could drive the car straight away. Without this car it is unlikely that we would have been able to function long term. As well as facilitating our work and making us independent it gave us great pleasure by enabling us to explore NE Thailand when we had some spare time.

There was a washing lady who washed clothes for other people at our accommodation block and she happily did our daily wash, returning each evening what we had put in for washing at 8.00 am in the morning.

With day to day living arrangements catered for I was able to settle into a daily work routine. However, it was not very clear how the Research Institute could facilitate the establishing of a faculty of pharmacy even though there was a lot of potential overlap with the Institute and the proposed Faculty in the area of herbal medicine. Everyone was not enthusiastic about my appointment as Director of the Institute and although not voiced openly in discussion, in fact the opposite, there was neverthe-less quite a bit of non-cooperation or even open opposition. We thought of the Thai proverb describing people "Speaking politely but wishing in their heart to cut your throat" and hoped that none of that type was around. Once, while we had been visiting another university, the Dean of Engineering had been murdered by contract killers, so we knew that nasty things could happen even to academics. Quite strong opposition was revealed when the suggestion was made that the Research Institute might be renamed the Walai Rukawej College of Pharmacy. A letter was secretly written to senior civil servants, thought to have influence with the royal household, suggesting dishonourable decisions were being made by the university authorities concerning the Research Institute and suggesting that this matter should be formally investigated. Perhaps fortunately and even rather amusingly the letter was sent to the wrong official department. Despite some dissent by a few, most of the staff were very helpful and openly committed themselves to the support of the ongoing work of the Institute and were excited at the possibility of reviving the Project to Establish a Faculty of Pharmacy.

There were days of frustration, however, when work did not proceed quite as planned. One Saturday afternoon was one such occasion and it brought out a non-Thai strong reaction on my part which caused a little stir. I was working alone on Saturday afternoon so that I could have the use of a computer that was connected to the internet. The internet connection proved to be so slow that it frustrated all my efforts to do what I had set out to do. It was so slow it kept getting timed out before making a connection. Or, perhaps having achieved some initial connections, it was eventually timed out before the desired website was reached. Having tried many times I eventually decided to give up and go home. It was about 4.30 pm and still quite light. Sunset was not until around 6.00 pm. When I walked down the two sets of stairs to the exit I found that a metal pull down door, like those used to lock up shops, had been fastened in place so that I could not get out. The door should not have been locked so early and in any case it was the responsibility of whoever locked the door to first check that no-one was working in the building. I thought to myself that I had no wish to be shut up there for any longer than necessary. Returning to the open corridor on the third floor I called for help to a guard on duty at the gate of the main entrance to the university about 50 yards away. The guard, understandably, found the situation a little amusing but was rather dismissive and did not offer any help saying that he could not open the locked door because he had no key. He then turned to walk away. I was somewhat annoyed and shouted to the guard that if he couldn't open the door then I would do it myself. I then went back downstairs and grasped the bottom of the gate and gave it a stiff upward jerk at the same time pushing hard with my right shoulder as low down the door as possible. The door began to buckle outwards and some more shoulder work created a gap at one side big enough to stoop under. Before that incident the door was not looking too healthy and rather the worse for wear, but after being buckled it was no longer usable and had to be replaced. On Monday I was asked some questions by a rather puzzled Dr. Sangkhom. He obviously thought I had been quite unreasonable. This is possibly so. He would certainly have tackled the problem differently, but then the guard would have responded far more positively to a vice-president of the university. Something I often experienced in Thailand was that, if a person was in a direct line of authority to me then they would be very polite and respectful, but not usually so otherwise. For example, this happened with students. If I was waiting for a lift and a whole group of students from another faculty such as Science, Humanities, Engineering etc., arrived at the lift after I had, then they would unconcernedly push their way onto the lift when it arrived until it was full and then leave without me. If, however, pharmacy students were present then they would show normal politeness and be concerned that I got onto the lift. Guards mostly acted similarly. If you were unknown to them they could ignore you completely. Ajarns (lecturers) would invariably be polite and those in service industries such as restaurants and hotels would also be most helpful and polite.

One of our biggest frustrations in Thailand is that we do not have an automatic feel of the Thai concept of time, particularly in relation to the commencement of meetings and the keeping of appointments. Time is something which becomes part of our mindset as we grow up and we get used to an accepted pattern of behaviour. Different behaviour tends to throw us. One day during our first few weeks at MSU the President said to me that he would like me to go with him and a group of staff to the town of Udorn Thani. This was about a three and half hour journey away by road. Amongst other things, there was a person there who would be useful for me to meet because he had a personal interest in the development of a Faculty of Pharmacy at MSU and could have some helpful ideas. The mini-bus would leave next morning at 5.30 am. I checked to make sure that it was at 5.30 am, and not sometime later like 6.30 am, and was told that if I arrived at 6.30 am the mini-bus would have gone. Next morning I was up at 4.30 am and trundled out in the old pickup truck to the front of the President's building on the old campus arriving about 5.20 am. No-one was there. The next person arrived at 5.50 am and others arrived at intervals after that. At 6.10 am the mini-bus arrived but shortly after the driver decided to go and collect the President from the centre of town. At 6.20 am the President arrived in his car and at 6.30 am the empty mini-bus returned. The mini-bus then had to go and fill up with diesel. At 6.40 am we set out for Udorn Thani. The time of departure evoked no comment from any of the passengers but left me thinking. "I knew that this was how it would be, but I did not have the confidence to turn up 'late'." There were numerous similar experiences but on one occasion at a later date I decided that I would act differently.

We planned to have a seminar one Saturday to discuss the way forward in starting the Faculty of Pharmacy. Speakers and participants would be invited, mainly from NE Thailand, including from the Faculty of Pharmacy at Khon Kaen University. It was hoped that our President would open the seminar by sharing with us his vision for the new faculty. This was doubly appropriate because not only was Dr. Pavich the President of MSU, he was also the best known pharmacist in Thailand. He was President of the Pharmacy Council, former Dean of the Faculty of Pharmacy of Chulalongkorn University and former Chairman of the committee of deans which constituted the Thai Consortium of Pharmacy Faculties. He was also very active in developing the practice of pharmacy in Thailand. Subsequent to the arranging of our seminar Dr. Pavich was required to attend an important government meeting on that same Saturday. He kindly offered to speak to our staff and any visiting speakers, who might have arrived, on the Friday evening. We would gather for a meal at 7.30 pm and then Dr. Pavich would speak to us. That Friday was a busy day for me and I thought to myself that the meal would probably start late so it would not matter if I arrived at 8.00 pm. On the law of averages that would have been the case but on this occasion the meal must have started promptly. When I walked through the door where the meal was being held everyone was sitting eating at several tables around the room. Dr. Pavich, and two visiting speakers were at a table to themselves at the far end of the room. All those at the other tables immediately stood to their feet and politely greeted me with a "wai" (hands clasped as in prayer in front of the chest with a slight bow of the head and smile if appropriate) and a broad smile. Dr. Pavich smiled broadly and invited me to sit with him. "Horrors," I thought, "I've got it wrong again". They all seemed to enjoy my embarrassment, although nothing was said and no-one really minded. Nevertheless I had got it wrong again. So you may understand a little why I had confusion with timing. A general conclusion I made, which nevertheless does not apply to absolutely every situation, is that the correct time for a meeting or an event to take place is when the most important person has arrived. If you are not the most important person you should arrive early, or be in close mobile phone contact with someone who is organising the meeting, or accompanying the most important person.

It was decided that courses in the area of public health would be a worthwhile activity for our faculty and have immediate benefits for facilitating the development of the faculty. The Public Health Service reaches to all levels of society in Thailand. In NE Thailand there are over 20 million people and so there were many thousands of people employed in the health service. There was a Public Health College in Khon Kaen, that had a two year diploma course in Public Health and many public health workers had this qualification. These people were limited in their job prospects, but if they could obtain a bachelor degree in public health (BPH) the possibilities for advancement as public health workers would greatly increase. Therefore it was decided that the proposed Faculty of Pharmacy should develop a two year course in public health which would enable those who already had a diploma to study further and obtain a bachelor degree. The course would have to be taught at the weekends in order for the public health workers to be able to attend. This would mean that it was a 'special course' and higher fees could be set for such a course because it would be delivered outside normal university teaching time. Such a course could well provide the finance the Faculty would need to pay lecturers for teaching public health and pharmacy. This then became part of our faculty plan and Sunantha, who had a Masters degree in Public Health, was asked to head up this development with the help and cooperation of two lecturers, Songkhramchai and Terdsak, from the Khon Kaen Public Health College. It was planned that the first intake for this course would be in June 1998 and that the two lecturers would transfer to MSU at the beginning of the next financial year in October and become a part of the Faculty of Pharmacy staff.

In mid March we returned to Aberdeen. Our original visas expired at the end of March and when we booked our flights we were unsure whether we would be granted extensions beyond the end of March. Nevertheless, as has already been mentioned, we were able to renew our visas in March until 30 September. Armed with those visas and Multiple Re-entry Documents we knew that we could travel home and return to Thailand again at our convenience. The undergraduate students' vacation is the period mid March until the beginning of June. It is also the hottest time of the year with day time temperatures in the upper 90s Fahrenheit and sometimes rising as high as 104° F. It was quite convenient for us to be away at that time and we also wanted to wait until the staff accommodation block was really ready for occupation. When we were due to return in May, friends at Khon Kaen University, Drs. Aroonsri and Sommai Priprem offered to go over to Mahasarakham and check if the accommodation was now ready. We decided to fly back to Thailand on Friday 15 May and stay the weekend at the OMF Home in Bangkok. This gave us the opportunity to phone our friends and again check the state of preparedness of the condominium accommodation. They told us it was still not ready for us to move into, no water for example, and suggested that it would be better if we postponed our travel to Mahasarakham until 28 May in order to allow more time for necessary building work to be completed. It was not possible for us to stay at OMF for more than about three days so we arranged to take a break in Huahin, on the Gulf of Thailand, about 100 miles southwest of Bangkok. We had enjoyed happy family holidays at Huahin in the 1960s but it had changed considerably since then. On Wednesday 20 May we travelled by a rather dilapidated train to Huahin and so to the Sofitel Central Hotel. This had previously been known as the Railway Hotel and was one of Thailand's original and best known hotels but was quite reasonably priced. To our surprise, no transport was waiting at the station to transfer us to the hotel. We had got too used to travelling by air! Most hotels would have their mini-bus meet all planes at local domestic airports. It was obvious that the train was no longer the preferred mode of transport for most hotel guests. Most people now transferred from Donmuang international airport Bangkok directly to the hotels in Huahin by minibus, or used their own private transport if they lived in Thailand. Had we informed the hotel of the time of our arrival arrangements would have been made to have one of their drivers meet us with a minibus. We were still operating as in a bygone age. Nevertheless we were able to agree with the driver of a dilapidated bus/truck with bench seats in the back, parked near the station, to take us and our cases the quarter of a mile or so to the hotel. Hotel porters were rather surprised to see us arrive by such a vehicle. We looked forward to our unexpected break, hoping it would do us both good, especially Joan, who had been feeling unwell for several days. During our time there Joan continued to have headaches and a fever despite taking paracetamol or aspirin. This considerably restricted what we could do but did not completely prevent us enjoying the superb facilities. We returned to Bangkok on 26 May and then flew up to Khon Kaen by the 6.55 am plane on Thursday 28 May. At the airport we were met by a group of friends including Aroonsri, Supatra, (former PhD students and Khon Kaen University lecturers) and Sunantha and Methin (lecturers from MSU) and were driven straight to the Khon Kaen City hospital to see Supatra's husband and our friend Dr. Wittya Chadbunchachai. He was expecting us, in fact waiting for us on the front steps of the hospital, and had arranged for Joan to have a whole series of examinations and medical tests – accompanied most of the time by several of our lecturer friends. We then went on to MSU and started to settle into our eighth storey top floor flat in the new staff accommodation block known as "Condo 1". Sunantha very nobly moved into the fourth floor at the same time to help us smooth out any initial teething difficulties we might have living in the almost completed accommodation. It was several months before anyone else moved into the building because it was not really fully functional. Nevertheless it was preferable to our previous arrangement and the car we had been loaned previously was made available to us immediately. In fact we had been driven from Khon Kaen to Mahasarakham in that car.

The next day we were told that Aroonsri had phoned and left a message to ask us to go back to Khon Kaen on Saturday for further tests and to see Dr. Pisarn, a consultant physician who worked at the Khon Kaen University Hospital. He was a friend of Dr.Wittya. Initially we stayed with Supatra and Wittya in their new house awaiting the results of tests and scans. Special attention was being focused on the liver. We were able to give an account of what was happening by email to our daughter Megan, a paediatrician, and to church friends in Aberdeen. A feature of our time at Mahasarakham was the support we could have through emails, especially from Megan (almost daily when the equipment was functioning) and also Tom Scott in Aberdeen who kept an eye on our house.

On Tuesday, 2 June, Joan entered a private

room/ward for further observation and to have a liver scan by magnetic resonance imaging (MRI) to provide clearer imaging of liver cysts, which had been identified with an ultrasound scan. However, after three days she was discharged as an accident had occurred which affected the MRI equipment. A car had crashed into an electricity pole causing a power cut which resulted in the MRI computer crashing. The damage caused took several days to repair. This gives a little insight into the standard of some of the driving in Thailand and also about the positioning of poles carrying high voltage electric cables! The MRI scan the following week indicated that the cysts were not of recent origin and it was concluded that they were not the cause of the present problem. This was a relief but we still did not have a diagnosis. There were various infections that Joan might have contracted in NE Thailand but none of these could be diagnosed. A course of treatment for the most common infection was taken nevertheless. With lots of rest and treating the fever with six hourly doses of either paracetamol or aspirin Joan's health very slowly improved over the next three months. We noticed that the aspirin was more long acting in its temperature lowering effect than the paracetamol and concluded that the anti-inflammatory effect of aspirin was having some beneficial action in addition to its antipyretic effect on the cause of the fever. Paracetamol is not noted for having an anti-inflammatory effect and so its action in this situation was related solely to its antipyretic effect. Throughout this period of three months, or so, we were very dependent on God's help and enabling. We were greatly helped through our daily Bible readings and prayer times and the prayers of our Christian friends at home and in Thailand. For example, on Friday 29 May, when we received Aroonsri's phone call asking us to return to Khon Kaen for more tests and investigations our daily reading was in the third chapter of Acts. There we read of the incident when the cripple asked Peter and John for alms as they entered the temple gates in Jerusalem. Peter replied "Silver and gold I do not have, but what I have I give you. In the name of Jesus Christ of Nazareth, walk." The comment I wrote at that time in my daily record was "A wonderful story of healing. Joan too Lord!" God gives the gift of hope through Jesus Christ. This gives us an unshakable trust in His faithfulness and an expectation that He will keep the promises that He makes to us in His word at the time and place that they are appropriate. Not the least of His promises are those that promise that He will hear and answer our prayers. Pastor Nipon, of the Khon Kaen Chinese Church and one of the church leaders Miss Suchitra (a lecturer in the Faculty of Nursing), visited Joan in hospital and prayed with her on the morning it was planned to try and remove a sample from one of the liver cysts. In the event it was decided it would be better to obtain better images of the cysts using MRI. Once these were obtained it was decided that the cysts were not of recent origin and so there was no point in proceeding with trying to obtain a sample of cyst contents. This was an important development and we would say that the decision not to aspirate one of the cysts was not unrelated to the prayers that had been made that morning. We were particularly concerned that the aspiration could have resulted in the need for a blood transfusion and this would have led to worries about HIV contamination. In the event we were guarded against such complications. Many tests still continued particularly trying to track down a possible infection. Could it be TB, Mellioidosis, or a fungal infection?

In the middle of all this we had the sad news by email from Megan on Sunday 13 June that Joan's Mum had died peacefully at 7.30 pm UK time on Saturday. This was not unexpected but it was an added blow to Joan who at this time was in the middle of medical investigations and not fit enough to travel home for the funeral. Communication with Megan was by email and with John her brother by air mail. The minister who led the funeral service was especially sympathetic about Joan's absence and made a point of saying so. He had been a missionary and had experienced a similar situation himself. This was helpful in mitigating the effects of Joan's absence at that time. We saw this as another instance of the Lord's overruling and provision in circumstances beyond our control.

The prompt and caring medical attention Joan received and the care and concern of our Thai friends was a great help to us. Many visited Joan during the time she was in hospital and their constant support made the stay in a Thai hospital much less strange than it might have been. I slept on a couch in Joan's private room and so was always nearby. The generous provision of their guestroom and liberal hospitality by Supatra and Wittya, whenever required, was also greatly appreciated.

Most of the tests which had been carried out on Joan were repeated when we were next home in Aberdeen but still no diagnosis was made. The question of what had caused the problem had to be left unanswered.

CHAPTER 3

DEVELOPING A WORKING FORMULA

In the late 1980s the government of Thailand
supported a large educational programme to
upgrade the teaching and practice of pharmacy in
Thailand. As part of this initiative a Thai-American
Consortium was formed between the Faculties of
Pharmacy in Thailand and many of the Colleges of
Pharmacy in the USA. The main part of this
programme was the support of Thai lecturers to
undertake PhD and PharmD studies in America. In
addition there was support for shorter training
programmes, visits of American academics to
Thailand to give lectures and advice and a two yearly
conference alternately in Thailand and America. This
was attended by representative staff of all participat-
ing faculties/colleges. (Arrangements were also
made between the Thai Consortium of Faculties of

Pharmacy and individual Schools of Pharmacy in the UK for Thai lecturers to undertake PhDs. The School of Pharmacy, The Robert Gordon University, was one of the main UK participants.) A meeting of the Thai-American Consortium took place in Chiang Mai, 24-27 June, 1998. This seemed to be a good opportunity to get some help for the MSU situation, particularly as the Thai Consortium, represented by their deans, had already made the decision that all pharmacy courses in government universities would move to a six year Doctor of Pharmacy (PharmD) curriculum by the student intake of June 2003.The PharmD is the qualification for entry to the pharmacy profession in the USA offered by all American Colleges of Pharmacy. It is not a true doctorate in that it is a first degree and not a higher degree like a PhD. In the American situation it was intended to be the equivalent of the American MD (equivalent to the UK, MB BS), which is also a first degree and not like the MD in the UK which is a higher degree. Nevertheless the American recipients of the PharmD are given the title doctor. This rather unsatisfactory confusion of the use of the title doctor in America was now in the process of being transferred to Thailand. Furthermore I would be involved in developing a PharmD programme. Rather ironic because I had argued against the introduction of the PharmD into the UK situation!

In 1998 the Thai government no longer had funds to provide new scholarships for Thai lecturers to undertake PhD studies in America, so we could not hope to negotiate such through the Consortium. Other less expensive forms of cooperation needed to be worked out. I hoped that one or more American colleges of pharmacy would give MSU some of their course materials. No one was prepared to offer this type of help and from the American point of view this was understandable. An academic institution cannot afford to spend money developing materials which it then gives away. In this case, however, those same institutions had already received fees from dozens of Thai students undertaking their courses. Giving us some course material, in that context, would be more of a gesture of goodwill and continuing cooperation than an act of financial irresponsibility. Be that as it may, Dr. Pavich had independently been having discussions with the Dean of the University of Florida, College of Pharmacy. As the result of those discussions Dean Bill Riffie had already made certain proposals to Dr. Pavich. These proposals would be discussed with me when Bill Riffie and representatives from two other American Colleges of Pharmacy visited MSU on Sunday 28 June.

The Florida proposal was along these lines. MSU should select four or so pharmacists to undertake the Florida PharmD programme. These people, once trained, would then help act as tutors for other pharmacists in NE Thailand, who would pay fees to be enrolled on the Florida distance learning PharmD programme. However, most of their study and work placements would be undertaken in Thailand. This proposal was very much a long term programme, which involved considerable expense. MSU students, by and large, were drawn mainly from the poorest region of Thailand, so finance was likely to be a problem and numbers would be small. However, the greatest weakness to the proposal was that it did not do anything to help MSU to develop its own PharmD programme in the short to medium term. We could not proceed on that basis. Nevertheless it re-emphasised to us that any immediate progress was largely dependent on what we could do ourselves. Professor Ed Moreton, from Maryland College of Pharmacy, called in to see us after he had visited Ubonrajathani University, 100 miles southeast of MSU. Ed said he would try and collaborate with us in the future, once we got our course started, by providing student placements in the USA and possibly by arranging staff exchanges between the University of Maryland and MSU.

The day after our discussions with Dr. Riffie I attended a special meeting of the MSU Administration Committee. We were told that the government had proposed that all government universities in Thailand should make plans to change to become autonomous universities. This was a policy imposed on the government as one of the conditions for receiving a large loan from the International Monetary Fund (IMF) to help Thailand recovery from the financial crisis of June 1997. All government university lecturers were currently civil servants and all decisions made by universities as to curricula and future university development had to be submitted for approval to the Ministry of University Affairs. This was unnecessarily bureaucratic and removed academic independence from universities. Academic independence is seen to have academic benefits by most countries. Another important consequence for MSU of moving towards being an autonomous university was that new faculties planned at MSU would now have to be constituted as autonomous faculties. That is they would be required to be much more self supporting than the government funded faculties. This did not mean that there would be no government support for autonomous universities. When money became available the government would still be prepared to make equipment grants and grants for new buildings. New staff, however, and the running costs of the faculty that we hoped to establish would have to be funded from money earned by the faculty. In addition new lecturers would have a different status and be known as lecturers of the university and not government civil servants. The salaries of these staff could be greater than the government salary scales but the staff would not have some of the benefits of government servants. For example they would not automatically have free medical treatment for themselves and family members. Neither would they have the privilege of wearing, on official occasions, a military style white dress uniform with rows of medal ribbons and special decorations and coloured sashes as appropriate.

At this time Sunantha, Methin and I plus Aroonsri and Nusaraporn from Khon Kaen had some initial discussions to consider the proposed MSU PharmD curriculum (I had proposed a curriculum for discussion in June 1997) and ways that the proposed new faculty might generate income in order to be self supporting. These discussions continued on a regular basis for MSU based staff and sometimes Aroonsri would come and help explain official university procedures. The lack of a budget to build and equip a faculty building was in my mind a major problem but I was assured that temporary arrangements could be made until we received our budget. We were also told that we were top priority in the proposed building plans for the university and would therefore receive a budget very soon.

On the suggestion of the MSU President we decided to plan to start with a two year top-up PharmD course for pharmacists who had already completed a five year bachelor degree in pharmacy and were already practising as pharmacists. This would not require specialised buildings and laboratories but would require suitable hospitals and community pharmacies for practice placements. These did not exist at present in our region of Thailand and therefore needed a planned development programme to upgrade the practice of pharmacy in Mahasarakham Provincial Hospital and hospitals in neighbouring districts and in the nearby provinces. Sunantha, with her previous hospital experience, took responsibility for this programme. It reminded me of the situation in Glasgow in the late 1970s when I was Course Director of the MSc Clinical Pharmacy at Strathclyde University. At that time the new content of the teaching that we were seeking to provide and the course requirements for clinical practice placements stimulated the development of pharmacy practice in nearby hospitals.

Developing suitable practice situations in community pharmacy was not going to be easy. Mr. Kata, a Bangkok community pharmacist, who was well known for his clinical practice in his own pharmacy, was invited to act as a course advisor to help us in developing our curriculum and teaching community pharmacy practice. We also formulated the long term plan of developing university community pharmacies (Unipharm). These would provide pharmaceutical care for patients, act as models for other community pharmacists, provide practice placements for our students, stimulate research and generate income for the faculty.

At a slightly later date the idea of producing drinking water for sale (Unipure) in the university's own production plant was also considered to be a project worth developing. It would provide practical teaching in producing a high quality product for human consumption, provide benefits for the public and be a means of generating income. Two other faculties were also interested to have this as their own faculty project and so drinking water production was a development where we would have to compete with others for permission to proceed. It is interesting that the Thai government requires all government universities to make contributions to social development in addition to teaching and research. This project would fit that requirement. The other major area of Thai university policy is the support and development of Thai culture and religion. Religion is almost automatically understood to be Buddhism but this in fact would not preclude some other religious activity involved with a different religion. Buddhism teaches that all religions are good and this is a generally accepted view of the majority of Thai people.

It was about July 1998 that I requested the University to re-establish the Project to Establish the Faculty of Pharmacy with myself as its chairman and Sunantha, Methin and a newly qualified pharmacist, Chanya, as members of the project team. I also asked that we would be allowed to transfer a few support staff from the Walai Rukawej Botanical Research Institute to provide the initial administration support staff for the project, at least until the project developed to the stage where it could support its own establishment of administrative personnel. These Walai Rukawej staff would be staff who volunteered to move with us. My requests were granted and so from the beginning of the next financial year (October 1998) the Pharmacy Faculty Project was re-established. It was decided that the name of the faculty we were seeking to establish should be 'The Faculty of Pharmacy and Health Sciences'. Four support staff transferred to the project with us and we could not have progressed without their valuable expertise. At this time the project was nominally under the umbrella of the Faculty of Science and Dr. Wanchai, the Dean, was always interested in what we were doing and sought to give helpful support and encouragement.

Once this agreement to re-establish the project was in place we could negotiate for some accommodation space. The Faculty of Humanities and Social Sciences was the first faculty to be provided with its on faculty building on the new campus. This was called the Rajanakarin Building. It was a large seven storey building and there was space available which was surplus to the Faculty of Humanities initial requirements. The Faculties of Engineering and Nursing, which were the last two newly developing faculties to receive government funding, were allocated space in the Faculty of Humanities until their own faculty buildings were ready. After some hesitancy the Faculty of Pharmacy and Health Sciences were allocated about half of the fifth floor of the Rajanakarin Building. This was used for a Faculty Office, Dean's office, open plan rooms for lecturers, seminar rooms, a meeting room and a room to develop a Medicines Information Service. There was also a large lecture theatre. Some internal alterations were needed and furnishings and equipment including air conditioners had to be bought and fitted. This was completed in time for us to move into in September 1998 and this was to be our faculty base for the next three years.

In July - August I was involved with the process of obtaining a year long contract with the university. We thought that this would help us to obtain 12 month visas and work permits. However, we were unsuccessful in our applications for visas at Nong Khai, as previously mentioned. Instead we only obtained three month visas, and so I could only get a three month work permit. We found this very disappointing and temporarily made us somewhat fed-up with Thailand. However, having obtained visas until January 1999 we decided to take another break back in Aberdeen leaving MSU in mid September. This precipitated a very busy week or so of activity in order to prepare for the period when we would be away. Sunantha would be responsible for the Faculty while I was away in Britain.

Our flight to Aberdeen via Amsterdam from Bangkok was 11.25 pm on 17 September, but we flew down to Bangkok on Friday 11 September. This was so that we could do some work for MSU and have a few days break before our long flight home. When I taught in the Pharmacy Faculty in Chulalongkorn University, Bangkok, (1965-1969) we had lived in the area known as Bangrak. This included the Silom Road, which developed as a commercial and tourist area over the years after we left. For us this area has a familiar friendly feeling to it and so we always like to stay somewhere near Silom Road, if possible. We also liked to take the opportunity of meeting up with friends, often at church, with whom we had kept contact with from our time in Bangkok. These were mostly former students who were now well established in their professions. On Saturday Mr. Suwatt Jitarawej took us for a tour round Bangkok. Suwatt and his wife Yenjai often insisted on taking us out for meals and a favourite place for us all was the buffet at the Novotel Hotel, Siam Square. On Sunday, after church, Mrs. Ampiga took us out for a meal together with her daughter and also her younger sister plus her three daughters. Suwatt, Yenjai and Ampiga were all involved with student cell groups for Bible study and fellowship with which we were also involved when we were in Bangkok. As well as being a part of on campus Bible study groups they also visited our home for special meetings and we got to know them very well. Suwatt now held a senior position in telecommunications, Yenjai was the senior manager of Siam Pharmaceuticals and Ampiga worked in the pharmaceutical industry in product registration.

Mr. Sopon was at that time the current General Secretary of the Thai Christain Students (TCS) organisation which developed from those original fellowship, prayer and Bible study groups. He invited me to visit the offices of TCS on Monday 14 September to talk to TCS staff about how the work began in the 1960s.

On Tuesday, Sunantha came to the Bangkok Christian Guest House, where we were staying, and then drove me to visit Mr. Kata, mentioned above. This was a good opportunity for me to see his community pharmacy and to have discussions with him. I was very impressed with what I saw. One of the services which Kata offered his patients, when they committed themselves to receive their medicines from him, was that he kept a complete record of all their medication and also of their medical history. If the person should need to enter hospital he supplied them a printout of these records. It was a fairly unusual situation for patients to have such complete records and the hospital staff would be very appreciative. Patients in Thailand may attend more than one doctor and possibly the doctors concerned would be unaware of this and be unaware of what the other doctor had prescribed or the tests he had ordered. Thus many doctors would not have full medication or full medical records. The patients would get a set of records from each doctor and allow Kata to make copies and this would give Kata a full picture of their medical and medicines history including their current treatment.

When we passed through Bangkok as we travelled in or out of Thailand, Joan and I would like, if possible, to go to one of the many first class hotels for a very modestly priced meal or snack. An especial treat would be a fruit drink, or a snack, sitting on the riverside terrace of one of Bangkok's original hotels, the Oriental Hotel, not so modestly priced! There we could watch the ferries crossing the Chao Phrya River, the clusters of big barges being towed on long lines by small tug-boats, the long-tailed boats and river taxis speeding up and down and the sun setting beyond the far bank. Afterwards we could sit in the lobby of the hotel for half an hour or so listening to the resident string quartet, playing snatches of classical music, but largely ignored by the hotel clientele dashing in and out about their business. Then we could walk or take a taxi back to whichever place we were staying.

Thursday, September 17 soon came and the time for our return flight home. Mr. Preecha, another friend from his pharmacy student and group Bible study days, who was then a consultant to certain food and pharmaceutical manufacturers, had offered to drive us to the airport in the evening. But it rained very heavily as he was driving to collect us, and this caused him to be held up in the traffic, so he phoned suggesting that we should not wait for him but take a taxi to the airport instead. I had first got to know Preecha when I was on a five day tour of NE Thailand and Laos with fifth year pharmacy students in 1968. He sat next to me on a coach one day as we were travelling and said that if I showed him my palm he would tell me my future. I said I could tell him something much better than that. When he asked what that might be I explained to him about Jesus Christ and what He had done for him. Preecha was very interested to learn more so I promised to get him a Thai New Testament. Later I went round to his home in Bangkok which had a shop front onto a main road. It was only 10 minutes walk from where we lived at that time and just across the road from a large fresh market where I often bought various items of food. Preecha was not at home at the time, so I left the New Testament with a member of the family, asking him to pass it on to Preecha. Some years later Andrew Way, an OMF missionary, who carried on and developed the work with students after we left Bangkok, told me that Preecha's brother, Mr. Watana, read the New Testament, became a Christian and later became a full time Christian Minister. When we have met Preecha in Bangkok in recent years he has told me that his father and mother also became Christians and about seven of his brothers and sisters. When quite young I read a missionary story from China illustrating the influence that reading the Bible can have on a person's life. The story told about a dog getting hold of an old tattered book from a pile of rubbish and running off past the guards into an army camp with the book in its mouth. Inside the camp the dog lost interest in the book and dropped it near a young soldier who picked it up and found it to be a Chinese New Testament. He read it and as a result he became a Christian. I can remember thinking at the time that this was a wonderful story but I would probably never experience anything like that. Well I was wrong.

I have learnt gradually in the Christian life that if I get an inner conviction that something should be happening, but it does not look as though it is going to happen in the normal course of events, then this might be a prompting from the Holy Spirit challenging me to specifically ask God to do it. An example of this happened to me quite strikingly on my first visit to China in 1983. I had gone to China with a tour group, but had arranged that once in China I would follow my own programme of visiting Pharmacy Colleges in Beijing, Nanjing and Shanghai. This was permissible and I had the necessary letters of invitation from each place. I agreed that I would meet up with the tour group again in Shanghai when we were all due to fly out to Hong Kong together. Travelling to Nanjing after being in Beijing for a few days I said to the Lord 'It would be good to meet a Chinese Christian. Isn't it about time I met one?' In 1983 everything was strictly monitored and it was not at all easy for Chinese to speak freely to foreigners. The next day after having discussions with two Chinese leaders about my programme in Nanjing we were walking out of the building and one man went to weigh himself on a weighing machine in the corridor. The other took the opportunity to whisper in my ear 'I'm a Christian too.' I was thrilled. In our discussions I had insisted that my programme must allow me to go to church on Sunday and from that he had guessed that I must be a Christian. He took responsibility for seeing that I got to church and we became very good friends and we have kept contact ever since. Then again I was visiting America on one occasion and said to the Lord that I would like to be used in some way by speaking a 'word in season' to someone in need. On my last day I was sitting at a bus station café having a meal before travelling to the airport. A young man came and sat opposite me and said 'I think you must be a Christian because I saw you giving thanks before you ate your meal. I have been asked to go home because a problem has arisen and they want me to return to help them but I'm worried because I don't feel that I can really help them. Can you give me any advice?' His bus was about to go in a few minutes, so there was very little time, but Isaiah chapter 50 verse 10 immediately came to my mind, especially the second part of the verse, which I quoted to him from memory. 'Let him who walks in the dark, who has no light, trust in the name of the Lord and rely on his God.' I encouraged him to follow this advice and made sure he had a note of the scripture reference. Then he was straight off on his way and I was off to the airport and my flight home. I think we both left feeling strengthened and encouraged. That was a very special experience for me because I realised it was the Lord answering my request and He gave me great joy in knowing that He was using me in His purposes to help a fellow Christian I had never met before. A little like Philip with the Ethiopian official (Acts 8:26-40.).

Joan was now feeling back to normal. As we walked through the Don Muang airport I noticed that she had a renewed zip in her step and commented that I, plus our hand baggage, was having a hard time keeping up with her. We were both very pleased about this and were looking forward to the journey. The flight to Amsterdam went well and we arrived on time just before 5.30 am local time. Then we were onto the moving walkways where we were chattering away, Joan in front of me but turned to face me. Before either of us had time to notice we had reached the end of the walkway and as Joan's feet hit the stationary edge she was thrown up into the air and twisted through 90 degrees so that she fell heavily onto her left side and was unable to get to her feet straight away. My initial reaction was. "Oh no, I hope that she hasn't injured herself badly, just after recovering from over three month's illness!" I was horrified to think that she might have broken her femur and be seriously affected. Joan was initially in considerable difficulty, and was unable to get up for about 20 seconds, but then recovered enough so that she was able to get onto her knees. I knew by then that at least her femur was intact. Then, rather gingerly, and with the help of a fellow passenger and me on either side of her, she was able to stand up. Her left groin was painful, her left elbow had been banged and grazed and she was quite shaken. We were both very thankful that she could walk and we made our way to a central service area and sat down and recovered with drinks of coffee before making our way to catch our 7.30 am connecting flight to Aberdeen. Joan was able to carry on fairly well although now slowed down and suffering pain as a result of the fall. Unfortunately, on this occasion instead of walking on the level to the departure gate, we had to walk down an awkward set of stairs to reach our departure area. After arriving at Aberdeen we took a taxi home and were pleased to find the house in good order. A missionary family, known to us, had stayed in the house for about six weeks while we were away and it had worked out very well. Then the usual re-entry activities were followed, getting in shopping, working through accumulated correspondence and trying to deal with the most urgent, getting the house in running order and contacting family. Joan was feeling quite stiff in her left groin but she carried on. Early Saturday morning I had the RAC call-out service mechanic come and replace my car battery which had run down completely in our absence. By 9.15 am the car was ready for use and as it was a lovely day we drove along the North Deeside road to Banchory for lunch. In the evening we were given a friendly welcome by the people attending our church prayer meeting and I was invited to give a brief report of the highlights of this last visit to Thailand. Our daily Bible reading that Saturday included these very encouraging verses.

'I tell you the truth,' Jesus said to them, 'no-one

who has left home or wife or brothers or parents or children for the sake of the kingdom of God will fail to receive many times as much in this age and, in the age to come, eternal life.' Luke's Gospel, chapter 18 verses 29 and 30.

There is an inevitable sacrifice, especially for family, when a person leaves home in response to God's leading. This is accentuated by the misunderstandings that can result, particularly on the part of those who may not have the conviction that seeking to follow God's will is the most important principle in life. It is comforting to know that the Lord Jesus not only knows about this, but that He is able to work these situations out for blessing. Nevertheless it is painful at the time and the pain may remain for many years. That has been our experience and that of our children. Although it is much easier for us and our family now, than when we had to separate when the children were young, it is still not easy.

The next few days I was involved in discussions with Drs. Dave Durham and Iain Liu who were continuing to work on a research project that I headed up while at RGU. I also had discussions with Mr. Griangsak as I was his main supervisor for his PhD studies. When I was in Thailand we kept in regular contact by email. On Friday Joan and I drove down to Lytham St. Anne's, to visit our daughter Megan and family for a long weekend. Megan is a Consultant Paediatrician and felt that Joan should have a medical opinion on her stiff groin resulting from her fall. On Monday 28

September she arranged for Joan to visit the Casualty Department of Victoria Hospital, Blackpool to see Mr. Harrop, a Consultant in Accident and Emergency. He suspected a fracture and the X-ray film showed that Joan had fractured the left anterior pubic ramus bone of her pelvis. No specific treatment was required. It was recommended that she continued to take exercise by walking but that she should take special care going up and down stairs. Again we were very thankful to God for His overruling that Joan had not been completely incapacitated by her heavy fall.

We suspect that Mr. Harrop informed Schiphol airport authorities of the accident, because we have subsequently noticed that there is now a voice warning 'Mind your step!' repeated several times before one reaches the end of the moving walkways.

Back in Aberdeen a statutory Ministry of Transport (MOT) road worthiness test for the car was due and the central heating system required its annual service. It was also time for our next prayer letter, Strategic Prayer Letter No. 48 to be written and sent out. The purpose of this letter was to indicate to our friends how their prayers for us over the previous few months had been answered and to mention some of the things we hoped to be involved with over the next few months. This was so that they could pray for God's guidance and blessing for us, and those we worked with, and that His good hand would overrule in all the various things we sought to do. We believe that prayer forms the essential basis of our work because we not only believe that God answers the prayers of those who seek to live according to His will, but that without His involvement in what we are doing we can do nothing worthwhile.

Then there was a paper on our research at RGU to be written together with colleagues for sending off for publication. In addition return flights needed to be booked for about the end of November. We prayed that we would be guided in this process and in particular that we would know the period of time that we should spend in Thailand. Buying the tickets was a step of faith that we would be fit and well on the date of departure. This was especially the case this time after the difficulties that Joan had experienced with her health in Thailand on our last visit and during our time at home as the result of her fall. We do not take out travel or health insurance for these visits. One reason is that the health cover is much less and the cost is much more for those of us 65 years and over compared with the cover for younger people. The other reason is we are much more familiar than the average tourist with the local health services available and have friends in health care provision. I am also a registered Thai pharmacist. With regard to travel insurance, the most common problem that occurs is misdirected or damaged baggage and in these situations we have found it much quicker and more satisfactory to deal with the airline direct than with an insurance company. On 12 October I booked our flights to go to Thailand on 30 November 1998 and to return to Scotland on 24 February 1999. Then we travelled about 1,600 miles by car to visit our sons and daughters and their families, and our two brothers (20 October-4 November).

CHAPTER 4

PROGRESS AND SHOCKS

After our return we had the opportunity, beginning in December, to provide our five lecturers and five support staff practice in English conversation and to help them improve their comprehension of written and spoken English. These are important skills which they all needed but which they had not had much opportunity to develop with native English speakers. We would often use an interesting newspaper article or a passage from the New Testament.

As it was approaching Christmas we used passages which dealt with the birth of Jesus Christ. This was a very interesting subject for conversation because they had not got a clear understanding of what Christmas was really about. 'Father Christmas' and 'The Foreigners' New Year', were the most common suggestions of the reason for Christmas. We also read and discussed parables from the Gospels as these provided useful knowledge and provoked interesting discussions. This English coaching by Joan went on for two or more hours a week throughout the whole of this visit and I joined in when I was able. We actually produced two books and many tapes to help our 'students'. One book was 'Polish Your English Skills' and the other was 'English for Research'. These were also used when we helped improve the English comprehension and conversation of PharmD students when they spent a week at MSU at the beginning of each new module of their course.

We were encouraged to be able to attend the Christmas services at the Khon Kaen Chinese Church. It was also a good opportunity for our friends at Khon Kaen to go to church with us. Quite a few Thais do take the opportunity of visiting churches at Christmas time to join in the special services and celebrations of Christ's birth and learn more about Him without feeling they are committing themselves long term. However, most of our friends declined our invitation with the excuse that they were too busy. Rather like the story Jesus told of the man who made a great feast and invited his friends, but they all declined with excuses that they had something very important to do, and so did not have the time.

It was during this next period in Thailand that I was responsible for finalising the PharmD curriculum and guiding it through the relevant university committees. It was formally passed by the University Council at its meeting held at Khon Kaen on 19 December 1998. This was potentially a very difficult meeting for me as I expected to be closely questioned on various aspects of the curriculum. Some of the scientific subject names in Thai were difficult enough for me without also having to be prepared to discuss the subject contents in detail with those wishing for further explanations as to why this or that was, or was not, included. I had also heard that certain members of the council, with an interest or teaching involvement in particular subjects, were going to raise their objections to certain aspects of the curriculum. This was particularly with regard to which faculty should be given the responsibility for the teaching of certain subjects. Such objections should have been raised, when the curriculum was discussed at the University Administration Committee, prior to being forwarded to the Council but no strong objections had been made at that time. However, these types of concern, regarding academic ownership of subjects having an overlap of content between two faculties, are often causes of friction between academics. This is especially so when discussing new courses of study and vying with each other for a share of the full-time teaching equivalents, and thus additional finance, resulting from increased student numbers. In my opinion the University Council was not the right forum for such discussions. Therefore it was both fascinating and a relief, from my point of view, that the meeting was chaired in such a way as to minimise my involvement and prevent any controversies arising which might be difficult for me. Mr. Meechai, the Chairman of the Council, was also Speaker of the Thai Senate, and it seemed to me he used some of his vast experience of chairing senate business in the way

he obtained the formal acceptance of the proposed
PharmD curriculum. When discussion of the curriculum came up on the agenda he asked, 'Does anyone
have questions to ask, or have any problems with the
proposed curriculum?' After a moments pause he
followed this with, 'Since none of you have any problems then I will ask some questions of my own. Why
is it necessary to study six years to become a pharmacist? I would have thought two years would be
enough. When I go to a hospital I never see a pharmacist. So why is it necessary to study six years to do
something which is seemingly so unimportant?' This
put the cat amongst the pigeons. Remember, Dr.
Pavich, the University President was a pharmacist.
There was also a council member, who was a medical
doctor, and he believed that the training of pharmacists needed expanding so that they could function
more competently in the clinical environment. These
two carried on a lively debate with Mr. Meechai, to
the enjoyment of the rest of the council. They
explained in detail why all the different subjects were
needed and how the modern role of the pharmacist
had changed in many countries and was now changing in Thailand. Several times I opened my mouth to
make a point, but I could not catch the chairman's
eye, or get a word in edgeways. After 20 – 30 minutes
Mr. Meechai reluctantly accepted that a six year
course was necessary after all. He then said that the
curriculum was accepted in its present form. Those,
who before the meeting were rumoured to have
certain objections, then said that they had some points
they wished to raise. They were told from the chair

that they had been given an opportunity earlier in the meeting to ask their questions and they had not said anything. It was now too late because the curriculum had just been accepted and we would now move on to the next item of business. Phew! Was that a case of God's overruling? We could now go ahead and advertise our two year top-up course for qualified pharmacists with a first intake in June 1999. It also meant that we must produce the major part of the fifth year course material as a matter of urgency. This material was needed in two formats. One format was for use as introductory material to the different modules and the other was for use in the distance learning mode.

At the beginning of January we had to start the process of applying for our visa and work permit extensions. I obtained the documentation needed from the university to lodge an initial application with the Labour Department on 6 January. This would be completed once we had our extended visas. Then we arranged for university transport to collect us at 6.00 am on Tuesday 12 January and take us to Nong Khai, so that we could apply to extend our visas until 30 September, when my one year university contract expired. Unfortunately the driver slept in so at 6.35 am we set off for Nong Khai in our own car and arrived at 11.30 am. Everything was almost in order. The bright young official we had encountered on our last visit said that the letter the university had written applying for a visa on our behalf was not in the accepted format. We persuaded him to phone the University External Affairs Department and explain to them how he required the letter to be written and then ask them to fax the approved letter to the Immigration office. Photocopies of the faxed letter were then required, but we were not able to use the photocopier in his office, so we were obliged find a commercial photo-copying service about a quarter of a mile away. When this was done and the visa and multiple re-entry fees were paid we had our precious visas together with permission to leave and re-enter the country during the life of the visa.

It was now time for some food before setting off on the return journey. We did not know much about Nong Khai but we opted to eat at the impressive sounding Grand Hotel. After eating and sitting there for a while we were convinced the hotel was wobbling, as though suffering from earth tremors, so we decided to leave as soon as possible! No we had not drunk the local whisky or rice wine! But perhaps all the excitement of the morning had given us wobbly legs!? We have not heard that the hotel fell down after we left! Our drive back to MSU went well and we arrived at 5.30 pm, about 30 minutes before sunset. On the way we passed the evidence of several road accidents. A frightening statistic is that three people are said to be killed every hour of the day on the roads in Thailand. At holiday times, like the International New Year, or the Thai New Year in April, Songkran, this is said to rise to five people every hour. About 80 % of these are motorcyclists.

In terms of the work of the Faculty, the next organisational milestone to be achieved was the formal establishment of the Faculty of Pharmacy and Health Sciences, as an autonomous faculty of the University. This was another meeting that I approached with much prayer and not a little trepidation. The formal agreement by the University Council was obtained at the meeting held on Saturday 13 February 1999. We praised God for His goodness and overruling in this whole exercise so that despite all the obstacles that had occurred along the way our academic commitment to establish a Faculty of Pharmacy at Mahasarakham University had been given official acceptance. It was only a beginning, and perhaps a very shaky beginning, but nevertheless a great step forward for pharmacy at MSU had been taken. A dean of another faculty of pharmacy, speaking publicly about three years later said, 'As far as I know, the Faculty of Pharmacy and Health Sciences at MSU had been established quicker than any of the previous faculties of pharmacy in Thailand.' Now we had to continue to develop courses, attract students and obtain finance in order that the faculty could fulfil its purpose. A special challenge for the new faculty was that we had to raise most of the money required for staff salaries and the general day to day administration of the faculty. On the positive side, we were already making good progress with income generation and in fact were able to purchase a seven seat Isuzu 4 x 4 as our faculty vehicle about that time. We could not afford to hire a specialised driver, however. This meant that the faculty vehicle had to be quite robust and passengers had to be quite strong nerved, as much of the driving was sub-standard. But that was not uncommon in Thailand.

After the establishing of the Faculty of Pharmacy and Health Sciences on 13 February we had just 11 days until our return flights to Scotland. Our plans for the faculty had worked out better than we could have expected and better than almost everyone we spoke to had expected. As already stated we believe that this was due to God's good hand guiding and overruling. It was now approaching the student long vacation, which in Thailand is March – May. You will remember that this is also the very hot time of the year with temperatures rising to the low 40 degrees Celsius in the day time and not falling below 30 degrees at night time. During this time more preparations would be made for the academic year beginning in June. Then the second intake to the two year top-up public health degree and the first PharmD intake to the two year PharmD degree would enrol.

We travelled down to Bangkok on Friday 19 February and stayed at the Bangkok Christian Guest House in Sala Daeng, just off Convent Road. It had originally been the home of Presbyterian missionaries and was the only remaining two storey residence, with a garden and lawn out front, in that street. Nevertheless, its days were numbered, as the pile driving for the foundations of a tall multi storey block right next to it had caused structural damage to the property and it would have to be demolished and rebuilt in the near future. Then we would have to stay elsewhere.

On Saturday we had done some shopping in the

morning and eaten lunch at the guest house. In the afternoon we took a walk along Silom Road and had afternoon tea nearby. When we returned to the house I needed to go up to the reception desk on the first floor to get the key to our room in the garden wing. Joan stayed downstairs and sat on a chair under the porch and rested her handbag on her knee. Before she knew what was happening a young man had come from behind her, snatched her handbag and dashed off down the garden path and out of the gate. There was a group of people sitting in the shade on the edge of the lawn but it all happened too quickly for them to be able to do anything. The guard who was usually sitting by the gate was occupied round the back of the house so the thief had no difficulty making his escape. I heard Joan shouting 'Thief' in Thai but arrived after everything had happened. Somewhat unsettling for Joan but fortunately there were no important documents in the handbag. There was a bunch of keys but I had a duplicate set so that did not cause us a problem. About £32 in cash was also in the handbag and that was it. Suwatt and Yenjai were taking us out for a seafood meal that evening and when they arrived they first took us to the local police station to report the theft. That having been done we were able to enjoy our evening together. Seafood is very popular in Bangkok and there are many such restaurants to choose from. Suwatt and Yenjai often amused us by discussing the merits of this or that restaurant, as they drove along, and which one would be the best for us. They were both very musical and would sometimes burst out into spontaneous singing of Christian songs. During the evening meal we could catch up with news. We could tell them something of what was happening at Mahasarakham and we were always interested to hear of their doings, particularly in relation to their church and their family. At that time Suwatt had just been appointed Chairman of the Board of the Yellow Bridge Chinese Church, Bangkok. This was one of the original churches to be founded in Thailand and had grown to be very large with a wide range of activities and had an influence throughout many parts of Thailand.

On Sunday we went to the Calvary Baptist Church with Dr. Mattana, who was a senior staff member in the Depatment of Pharmacology of the Faculty of Pharmacy, Chulalongkorn University. Mattana had been one of the key people involved with the founding of Christian Bible study groups and had for many years been Secretary to the Board of the Bangkok Bible College. Each Sunday afternoon she led a ladies Bible study group at another church. On Monday, Mattana took us a drive out of Bangkok to show us the fairly new International Campus of Mahidol University. In the evening we met up with Ampiga and her daughter Sisi. Then Suwatt took us out again on Tuesday. Preecha drove us to the airport on Wednesday.

It is obvious from the above that we were graciously taken care of during our time in Bangkok by Christian friends we had known for over 30 years from their student days. After a very good journey back to Amsterdam we flew on to Aberdeen and saw snow on the hills as we reached the coast of Scotland. Dr. Iain Liu research fellow, and Griangsak PhD student, met us with their cars at the airport. You may think we were spoilt and you would be right!

We quickly got back into the pattern of life in Aberdeen, contacting the family, getting the car running, shopping, attending to correspondence, medical for Joan, running the home, seeing to bills and matters to do with the house, linking up with friends at the church prayer meeting and services and discussing research matters in the School of Pharmacy. Mrs. Narumol, a staff member from Khon Kaen, who was approaching completion of her PhD at RGU was very concerned and unsettled that her PhD director of studies was to be replaced at a crucial stage in her studies. I was one of her supervisors and was also responsible for her coming to RGU in the first place and she was looking to me to help, but it was a very tricky situation for me to get involved with as an ex head of school. Despite some unpleasantness it was eventually resolved satisfactorily with her director of studies remaining unchanged. During this time it was also planned that Griangsak would have his PhD oral examination and his thesis was in the process of being written and needed to be checked.

The results of Joan's blood tests were still not back to normal from the time of her prolonged illness in Thailand and were causing her doctor some puzzlement. On Monday 8 March her doctor rang to ask that she arrange to give more blood so that the tests could be repeated once more. That day we read in the first two chapters of Exodus about the birth of Moses and the problems his parents faced in keeping him from being killed by Pharaoh. Then the step of faith his mother and sister took by floating him in a basket so that Pharaoh's daughter might see him and take pity on him. Their faith in God was rewarded. A comment on that passage in the daily Scripture Union Notes was; 'Focusing on our human predicament may paralyse us because the situation may appear humanly impossible. But concentrating on God and His power will help us see the way out.' We were seeking to look to God for His way through this continuing health puzzle. On Wednesday 17 March we heard that Joan's blood test results were considered to be moving towards normal and that no more tests would be necessary for the time being. The Bible reading on the next day included the verse, 'There the Lord made a decree and a law for them, and there He tested them.' Exodus 15: 25b, NIV. My written comment on that was; 'The Lord does test us to give us the chance to show that we are prepared to walk by faith and not by sight.' I also wrote; 'Great news yesterday that the medics have independently agreed, what we had already decided with Megan, that there was no point in Joan having further investigations at present. That opens up the way before us to return to Thailand! I believe the Lord has not only tested our faith but He has honoured our faith also. Thank You Lord.'

I was very involved with research matters at RGU for about two weeks and then we took a break by going on another very enjoyable 'grand tour' of our sons and daughters in various parts of England

(Wednesday 31 March – Monday 19 April).

When we returned to Aberdeen we had a surprise visit from two Thai Christian sisters, Miss. Tippawan and Dr. Woranoot. They were visiting England and wanted to take the opportunity of seeing us. Tippawan was spending several months gaining experience caring for children with disabilities in Cambridge and Woranoot had come to visit her. This was a very significant visit for Joan and me and for them, because over the next two to three years we saw each other several times when Joan and I passed through Bangkok.

Tippawan studied nursing at Chiang Mai and was greatly helped in her Christian life at that time by OMF Missionaries Theodore and Pam Welch. Theodore and Pam did their year of language study in Bangkok during the time we were living there when I was teaching in Chulalongkorn and seeking to help form Christian cell groups for Bible study and fellowship. We were very keen that other OMF missionaries would seek similar opportunities at universities in different parts of Thailand. Therefore it was thrilling for us when Theodore and Pam went to Chiang Mai and Theodore had the opportunity to teach surgery in Chiang Mai Univesity. After qualifying as a nurse Tippawan worked full time as the leader of the Hospital Christian Fellowship of Thailand. Now she was exploring the possibility of working in China helping and caring for children with disabilities. This eventually led to her heading up a teaching programme for combating Aids by seeking to change peoples' lifestyles. Woranoot had a PhD from an American university in the field of Education and was Vice Principal, soon to become Principal, of Bangkok Christian Boys College. This is the oldest, founded in 1852, and one of the most academically successful schools in Thailand. It also has the added distinction of having the best record for success in school football in Thailand!

Tom Scott took us to the airport on Monday 17 May. The flight via Amsterdam went well and we arrived at the OMF home Bangkok in time for a late lunch (1.00 pm). On Thursday we flew to Khon Kaen and then on by road to MSU arriving in the early afternoon and took over the car and the flat again. I was working as usual on Friday and soon into the normal round of university and faculty meetings, English language coaching and Sunday morning services at Khon Kaen Chinese church.

About twelve new lecturers had been appointed, mostly in Public Health, during our time away. It took some time before we really got to know them all. Increasing numbers of staff brought increasing administrative responsibilities. The somewhat remote location of the university meant that staff that possessed a PhD were almost impossible to recruit and staff with a Masters degrees were also very difficult to attract. This meant that most of our staff were young, just held a Bachelor degree and had no previous experience of teaching. The situation was further complicated by the requirement by the university that all staff that only possessed a Bachelor degree should be enrolled on a Master degree programme, within two years of taking up post, or the faculty would forfeit that member of staff. To get a person onto a Master degree programme at another Thai university involved finding suitable funding for them for up to four years. When they returned with their Master degree the staff member would then be pressing as hard as they could to get on a PhD programme! Of course two years should be long enough to undertake a Master degree, but in Thailand the supervisors of such students are in no hurry to get them through their studies. This is because the student provides a valuable resource for the supervisor in many different ways. Another problem which I met was that supervisors might take on more students than they had laboratory space and equipment to accommodate. (Of course such students would have more time to be useful to their supervisor.) Thus one student may have the use of the equipment for the first part of the day and another student for the second part of the day. Alternatively one student might work in the laboratory for several weeks then have to make way for another student to have the use of the facilities for an equivalent period. Not the most efficient system ever thought of! When I realised something of what was considered normal supervisory practise I made it known to both student and supervisor that the student could only have an extension to their two years away from MSU after a full explanation of the reasons had been given to me and had been accepted. If extra time was agreed it would be for six months only. After that if the student had not finished then they would be required to return to MSU and help with teaching and complete their write up concurrently.

This system was accepted as being a fair system because it theoretically meant that we could plan which members of staff returned when and consequently which times we could plan for other members of staff to proceed to further study. There was one big upset when one member of staff felt that he could arrange his own time for going away without consultation. That only reinforced the rule that everything was done with proper consultation and following the previously agreed timetable.

An interesting thing was that our phone in the flat was working at the time of our return in mid May and, not only working, but able to receive and send international calls. This was not usually the case and that had been a great source of frustration to us. Nevertheless it was working at this time. At 8.00 pm on Sunday 30 May, Rose our second daughter, phoned to say that we should phone Peter our eldest son, as he had some bad news to tell us. We immediately phoned him and he told us that Jan, his wife, who had left Peter and the four children (Laurie 14, TJ 13, Hugh 12 and Dicken 11) about 15 months before had been found in her home murdered. This was a very great shock for us all.

Next day we sent emails to Dominic Smart our minister in Aberdeen, Megan, KLM re changing our return flights and to cancel some tentative accommodation arrangements we had already made for the original dates of our return through Bangkok. Megan phoned at 10.00 pm that evening and encouraged us in what we were doing. KLM flights were unavailable for Friday 12 June, and we ended up booking seats for Monday 14 June but travelling to Bangkok on Saturday, 12 June.

We received a letter from Woranoot on Tuesday 1 June enclosing copies of photographs taken when she visited us in Aberdeen. Woranoot also invited us to stay with her at the Bangkok Christian College when we visited Bangkok. Little did she know that right at that time we were in the middle of trying to make arrangements to stay somewhere in Bangkok. We took her up on her offer immediately by phoning and arranging to stay 12-14 June. Her accommodation was only about 200 yards from the house we used to live in. The morning of that same day I was able to arrange a meeting with the University President. This was a minor miracle, as he was often away from the university. Furthermore when he was present it was very difficult to arrange an appointment with him because there was usually a long queue of people wanting to see him. He agreed that I could take leave from the university on 12 June to visit Peter. I phoned Peter on 1 June and told him what we had been able to arrange so far. The following Friday we wrote a brief letter to let our praying friends know about Peter's and our situation. We sent off 39 copies by air mail on Saturday morning from Mahasarakham main post office. Air mail letters could reach their destinations in the UK within three days if all went normally.

The first two year top-up PharmD intake were due to commence their course on Monday 7 June, when seven students would come to the university for five days to receive the introductory teaching for the first two modules of the course. They would then study for the next three months in their homes and places of work, but keeping in touch with the lecturers by email, phone and ordinary mail. It had been arranged for almost a year that I would take the responsibility for getting the course started and would be personally involved in teaching the first three days of the course. Therefore I felt that it was very important to make sure that one of the major objectives that we had been working towards for 18 months was officially up and running before we returned home. Starting the two year top-up PharmD course was also an important milestone to starting the six year PharmD programme the following June. Not until we had students enrolled on full time study could we really consider the faculty to be a fully functional faculty. The part time courses in public health and pharmacy were an essential stepping stone to achieving that objective and enabled us to get curricula, teaching materials, appropriate staff involvement, adequate finance, teaching and administrative facilities in place.

On Friday 11 June the University President Dr. Pavich phoned to tell me that he had signed the university authorisation making me the first Dean of the Faculty of Pharmacy and Health Sciences. This was good news for me to be made dean and it may still be unique for a foreigner to hold such a position in a Thai Government University. At the time it did not make as much impact with me as it should have done, but with time I greatly appreciated the honour. The President also again encouraged me to return to the UK for family reasons for as long as I felt it was necessary.

Before leaving on the Saturday morning I formally welcomed the second intake of 186 public health students to commence their two year top-up degree course. They studied at the weekends and so were just commencing their course on that Saturday. These welcomes to new intakes of students gave them an opportunity to know who I was and gave me an opportunity to publicly ask the God who was high overall and who created the heavens and the earth to bless them.

The journey to Bangkok and the stay with Woranoot worked out very well. Saturday evening Suwatt and Yenjai again took us out for a meal. On Sunday we went to the Yellow Bridge Church with Woranoot and afterwards went to lunch with her. Ampiga and her daughter Sisi, 16 years old, took us out for the evening meal and Ampiga prayed at length for our family when she gave thanks for the meal. On Monday Suwatt insisted on looking after us for lunch and then in the evening he and Yenjai took us out to the airport in their car. After a very good flight home Tom and Iain (Chinese Christian Post-doctoral Fellow) met us at the airport at about 8.30 am.

While still in Thailand Joan had indicated to Peter that we would understand if it was necessary for the funeral to take place before we got back and this is what happened. All of our family went, or were represented at the funeral. From our point of view, it meant that we could rest up and suitably recover from the journey before making the long drive to Peter in Lincoln. This had the added advantage that we were able to spend longer with him and his family because others who had been staying with him had then left. The evening of the funeral (16 June) we were in touch by phone with all of our immediate family after they had returned home, except Rose and Dave who had a longer journey, and heard how the day had been for each of them. We went down to Peter on the following Friday and stayed for two weeks. During that time we were able to have some overdue discussions with Peter, which although painful for us all, were very necessary in helping us understand each other better. Our grandchildren were suffering quite badly and were not interested in talking very much at that time. Nevertheless it was an opportunity for us and them to get to know each other better. Previous visits had always been shorter.

Our journey back to Aberdeen was via Megan and family in Lytham St. Anne's. When travelling between Peter and Megan, or Ann in Leicester and Megan, we often diverted from the quickest route to drive through Derbyshire to see what was happening to the places I knew in my early years. On this occasion we had a coffee break at Ashford in the Water, a charming little village about two miles outside Bakewell on the Buxton road. Perhaps at this stage I may also make a diversion back in time. Bakewell like the village of Ashover and its surrounding hills and the park around Hardwick Hall (the main army parachute training centre in World War 2) have always held a special attraction for me. In those war years (1939-45) when I was aged 6-12, Bryn, my older brother and Peter Wright our mutual friend used to range fairly widely on our bicycles from our home village of Morton, where we were born. I rode a very small two wheeler until I was about nine years old when I had an adult size bicycle with wooden blocks attached to the pedals so that my legs could reach them. Ashover and Hardwick might be visited in this way. We knew most of the twists and turns in the roads and lanes for several miles around. On foot we kept within a smaller radius of the village, although I can remember walking to Hardwick at least once after the war. Within a mile or two of home we were acquainted with every field and hedgerow, the best climbable trees, useful short cuts and places to hide. I used to imagine that I would be able to use my local knowledge of the terrain to carry secret messages if we became an occupied country! The stories of Robin Hood, which were popular in those parts, probably gave us false delusions of our capabilities. His exploits also entertained us and caused us to try and emulate his prowess with our home made bows and arrows and multipurpose quarterstaffs.

After the war we spent a lot of our time practicing and playing football and cricket for various teams. Bryn and I shared a tandem and when we went out rides we sometimes drew shouts from people we passed on the way that 'The one on the back's not pedalling!' Bryn sometimes thought that it only confirmed his worst suspicions! The summer when I was 14 we rode the 150 miles to Llanwrtyd Wells in Breconshire (my father's birthplace) in one day, and a few days later proceeded on to Pendine, near Tenby. There we were startled by a loud speaker bellowing at us, as we rode along the vast expanse of sands, that we were just about to enter a mined area! The journey home was less exciting!

We also got very involved in campanology. Both of us had been in the church choir since we were seven or eight years old so already had a lot to do with the church. A completely new ringing band was formed which originally consisted of six 16 year olds, plus myself, a 14 year old. We all belonged to the church Bible class which my father ran on a Sunday afternoon. All were very keen and we made very good progress, so much so that we made quite an impact in bell ringing circles in Derbyshire and Nottinghamshire, and even nationally. Bryn was the leader of the band, or the Ringing Captain of Morton Holy Cross Church Tower. He has become very well known for his ringing skills. One of his sons, Christopher, and Christopher's sons have followed in his footsteps. Joan's brother, John, and many of his family are also keen bell ringers in Surrey and neighbouring counties. After leaving home for university my ringing activities gradually tailed off but Bryn continued his ringing in London churches while at university.

Lasting impressions seem to be made by the scenes and familiar places of our formative years. I'm pretty sure that what we saw and heard in and around Hardwick, on those wartime visits, had quite an influence on me later when I had the opportunity to volunteer for parachute training during my National Service. Exploring the fields together, getting plenty of exercise, using our initiatives to devise our own entertainment and to get out of scrapes, had its influence and benefits too. The ability to use one's initiative, to accomplish something a little unexpected or out of the ordinary which was also beneficial, was a skill that was seen to be highly desirable and to be encouraged by those in leadership positions in the paras.

Back to 1999! Sunantha arrived in Aberdeen on Tuesday 6 July – the day after we arrived back in Aberdeen from visiting family in England – to develop her PhD proposal and to complete documentation to register for a PhD of RGU. I would help her in the preparation of the documentation and be her Research Director once her PhD was registered. This was quite a responsibility for me as most of the research would be undertaken in Mahasarakham and so there would not be a great deal of input from anyone else. The RGU regulations required that Sunantha spent a total of at least six months of her PhD registration period working in Aberdeen. Nusaraporn from Khon Kaen University was also undertaking a PhD with me in this same mode. Supatra, had also undertaken her PhD under this arrangement and completed it the day we left Aberdeen for Thailand in January 1998. The plan was for Sunantha to work in Aberdeen on this visit for two months and that meant that she would not return to MSU until the end of August. It was not a good idea for both of us to be away from MSU for too long so Joan and I were planning to return on 28 July. Meanwhile, as well as having quite a lot of commitments with research matters at RGU, including Narumol writing her thesis, we were able to enjoy some very nice summer weather in Aberdeen and show Sunantha around. Joan and I even ate out in the garden one day which was fairly unusual for us.

Tom delivered us to the airport on Wednesday 28 July and although our plane from Aberdeen to Amsterdam was delayed 45 minutes we just managed to make the connecting flight to Bangkok. After purchasing tickets for a flight to Khon Kaen on the following Monday we took a taxi to the OMF Home. There we were able to have a late lunch, settle in and relax. On Sunday we went to the Yellow Bridge Church and caught up with Suwatt, Yenjai, Tippawan and Woranoot. Then on Monday we travelled to MSU.

During this time at MSU I needed to ensure that the Faculty programme made progress in developing the drinking water project and the community pharmacy project. I would need to follow the procedure for preparing proposals within the university. The proposals would need to indicate the aims and benefits of the projects, especially the benefits to the community and the faculty, outline a strategy of how each would be accomplished, and provide a detailed statement of the costs involved. These proposals would first be taken to the Faculty Administrative Committee, then the University Administrative Committee and finally to the University Council.

The Council would then decide whether either or both of the projects could go ahead, or not, or whether more information was required.

Wednesday – Friday we wrote and sent out Strategic Prayer Letter No. 52 giving a summary of the important things that happened while we were home and mentioning, amongst other things, the above two projects which we hoped to progress during this time at MSU. We also included this sentence; 'Joan also has a project to get a washing machine and have it plumbed in to our kitchen if possible.'

The background to the above 'project' of Joan's was that since we moved into Condominium No.1 we had not had a satisfactory means of getting our clothes washed. Originally we were told that two girls who worked as cleaners in the building would wash our clothes for a certain amount of money. This did not prove to be a very good arrangement. Their standard of work was just about passable but their attitude was at best disinterested and at worst very rude. When more people moved into the condominium washing machines were provided on certain floors but not on the eighth floor. I asked a senior member of staff why there was no washing machine on the eighth floor and he replied, 'It is not appropriate for people such as a dean or their wife to do their own washing.' I thought it was even less appropriate for my wife to carry washing down to lower floors in search of a washing machine not in use. In a hot climate one changes clothes frequently and washing has to be done almost every day. As the building had more and more people come to live in it the situation was reached where the washing machines were always busy and people had to put their dirty washing in baskets and leave them in a queue in front of a particular washing machine. If the washing machine finished a cycle of washing and the owner of the clothes was not around the next person would open up the machine and take the washing out. This was not entirely satisfactory but what was worse was that there was so much washing to be done that the washing sometimes continued into the small hours of the morning in order for everyone to get their clothes washed. Then some machines ceased to function and the problem was compounded. That was why Joan had a project to get a washing machine!

Saturday morning, the day after our prayer letter went off, the President was attending a meeting at the university. After the meeting a meal was provided. I sat next to the President and was telling him all the things I was hoping to work on over the next few months. He mentioned that at the end of August all university budgets would be closed and he still had some money left in a particular budget which he wanted to spend. Did I have any suggestions on how he might spend some of the money? It made me think of Esther, backed by fasting and prayer, bringing her request for the safety of the people of Israel to the King (Esther chapter 4 verse 16), or Nehemiah prayerfully making his request to rebuild Jerusalem after the King asked why his countenance was sad (Nehemiah chapter 2 verse 4). Joan and I had already prayed about 'her project to have a washing machine' and so I brought up the subject of the need for a washing machine. I explained to Pavich how inconvenient it was for us getting our washing done under the present system and how it would make a great improvement to the efficiency of our living if we could have a washing machine in our flat. 'Oh, that's alright,' said Pavich, 'I can arrange that and I will get you a tumble dryer too.' We were very encouraged. Dominic Smart, our minister in Aberdeen, shared this answered prayer with the church Saturday evening Prayer Meeting and I heard that some of the ladies asked him jokingly, 'How can we get to talk to the University President?'

There were two other issues mentioned in that prayer letter No. 52 of August 1999. Our desire to be able to meet up with other Christians, staff or students, who were at the university and the need for new visas for us both and a work permit for me before the end of September.

The washing machine was delivered the following Wednesday which was very quick and encouraging. Those who delivered it wanted to connect it up and be off as soon as possible, but they had not worked out properly where the waste water would be discharged. They knocked a hole through the wall into the bathroom and thought that the machine could just discharge its water onto the bathroom floor and find its way out through the shower drain. There was also a problem that the outer casing of the washing machine was 'live' when the electricity was turned on. Just don't touch it when it was switched on was their solution. We thought that we had better contact Mr. Charoen, the university engineer who oversaw all kinds of instillations which were being made every day into the University buildings. He responded quickly and brought one of his workmen with him. Charoen muttered disapproval at the lack of know how of those who had delivered the machine. He told them, 'Discharging soapy water onto the bathroom floor used by old people like us would be very dangerous. It would cause us to fall down and break our bones. No, that would never do. What were they thinking of? They had better go away and leave it to him if that was the best they could do.' He then discussed it with the one he had brought with him and left him to plumb the outlet from the washing machine straight into a drain and include a breaker switch in the electricity circuit. It was nevertheless quite a few more days before we got the electric circuit functioning satisfactorily and the tumble dryer fitted with its own earth connection. The Thai system uses two point plugs and sockets with no earth connection.

During August I was working with faculty committees to try and finalise proposals for both the Unipharm and the Unipure project. We were also trying to determine what kind of a building the community pharmacy should have and looking for the best location in the centre of town. There were several locations which were suggested and considered but no sooner had we decided on a particular property to propose as a suitable property for renting than some obstacle arose. The President told us that there was a possibility of renting a piece of land which a relative of Charoen, mentioned above, owned. This was near to where it was being proposed that the night market, which functioned from about 5.30 – 10.30 pm, was to be relocated. At present the night market had completely taken over one of the main streets in the centre of town and this was unsatisfactory for many reasons, not least of which was because of hygiene considerations. A large part of the night market consisted of food stalls and small areas where people set up their gas heated semi-portable kitchen cookers to produce meals. Customers ate close by sitting at small tables. But the lack of running water made this undesirable. Night markets like this were very common in Thailand and this night market was very popular with the people of Mahasarakham, many of whom did not concern themselves too greatly about the finer details of food hygiene. In Thailand it is quite common for someone or some groups of people to set up market stalls and food stalls on a pavement, street corner, road or a convenient piece of apparently unused land, without permission. Others quickly join them and by the time the authorities decide that this is undesirable the traders are already established and object to being asked to move. The Thai way of handling differences of opinion is to avoid confrontation between officials and groups of the general public if at all possible. The resolution of the problem consequently proceeds very slowly. Another common factor which delays any corrective action being taken is that the traders pay a 'rent' to the local police who then allow them to stay where they are. (Another example of the lack of law enforcement, similar to the situation of the lack of enforcing measures that would result in improved driving safety.) In this particular case in Mahasarakham the city council was in the process of having the night market moved, to a former no longer used bus station, about a third of a mile away. The traders were making lots of complaints and threatening, either not to move at all, or if they were made to move, then they would move back to their former location at the first opportunity. Therefore there was an element of risk in our locating where we thought the night market would be in future. If we delayed then we would probably lose our opportunity, as other traders would wish to relocate their businesses or set up new businesses, near to where large numbers of people were soon expected to be gathering in the evenings.

Together with Dr. Pavich we decided on the following plan. The faculty, in the name of the university, would make an agreement to rent the land from Charoen's relative and we would build a portable pharmacy on that land which could, at least theoretically, be relocated if the need arose. A firm in Bangkok, The Siam Steel Company, had as one of its subsidiary enterprises the production of prefabricated single storey buildings, like petrol stations and similar retail outlets, which could be transported and assembled on any suitable piece of land in any part of the country. We began quite complicated negotiations with this company to see if they could produce us something to our design for not greater than one million Baht (£16000). We also began negotiations, through Charoen, to engage a local contractor to build a single storey building to our own design on the university campus, for the production of drinking water. This too should be for a sum not exceeding one million Baht.

The proposal explaining and requesting the go-ahead for the Community Pharmacy Project was submitted to the University Administration Committee on Tuesday 17 August. The community pharmacy was intended to provide: 1)an example, both in the physical design of the premises and the type of pharmaceutical care service provided, for other pharmacists who may plan to open a community pharmacy; 2) a teaching resource, both for teaching pharmacy students the factors involved in the administration of a community pharmacy and a practice placement location, where students could gain good community pharmacy practice experience; 3) a research resource for conducting pharmacy practice research and developing innovative practice; 4) a staff development resource, for lecturing staff to develop their knowledge and skills of pharmacy practice; 5) a source of income, to repay the original loan, to develop additional community pharmacies managed by the Faculty of Pharmacy and Health Sciences and to generate income for the faculty.

Our plan was to start with the community pharmacy in the night market area of Mahasarakham and then later to have another pharmacy on the university campus. Then, as funds became available, it was planned to open other pharmacies in nearby towns.

A plan was also put forward to build and equip a

drinking water manufacturing facility on the university campus. Potable water production would be based on the Reversed Osmosis (RO) principle. The equipment needed to accomplish RO was very expensive in the local context and we estimated that we would need a minimum of one million Bhat to equip the potable water production facility adequately.

In the two proposals which were produced we requested two million Baht for the Unipharm community pharmacy project. (One million Baht was for setting up each of the first two pharmacies with stock and equipment). One million Baht was also requested to purchase the equipment necessary for the drinking water project (Unipure). This was on the basis that we would get the equipment for a very competitive price by inviting several firms to submit competitive tenders. It was requested that the university agree to provide the money for the buildings for both projects, because the buildings would belong to the university.

Dr. Pavich had by this time negotiated the rental of the land, near the proposed night market, for the first community pharmacy. The Administration Committee duly approved our Faculty Proposal and referred it for consideration by the University Council at their next meeting which was to be to be held in Bangkok on 26 August. I travelled down the evening before and stayed overnight with the secretariat and council members from MSU who would be attending the council meeting commencing at 9.00 am the next day. After the meeting had been in process for three hours I was asked to join the meeting as the agenda item that I was concerned with had been reached. In the Lord's goodness I was not asked to make an oral presentation, in addition to the fully detailed written documentation, and no difficult questions were asked. After about five minutes discussion the Council agreed that three million Baht from a university revolving loan fund could be allocated to the two projects. In addition the university would finance the two buildings required.

Now we had to get on with the even more tricky business of turning both proposals into functioning realities. This meant that for both projects we would have to develop sustainable businesses that were capable of competing effectively in the market place. As a faculty we hoped that we would be able to open the community pharmacy in the market sometime during the next long vacation (March – May 2000) and possibly start producing drinking water a few months after that.

In terms of our time at MSU, and establishing the Faculty, the Council meeting in August 1999 represents a suitable time to pause, backtrack in time several decades, and consider our first connections with a Thai university and some of our experiences leading up to that.

PART II

PIONEERING AN EVANGELICAL CHRISTIAN STUDENT FELLOWSHIP

CHAPTER 5

INITIAL PREPARATION

I came to know the Lord Jesus Christ as my Saviour in a personal way in 1953 when I was a university student. The members of the small Christian Union at the School of Pharmacy, University of London, who I had spoken to, including my future wife, Joan, claimed to know God in a personal way. This was new to me. I believed in God and would have said that I was a Christian, but I could not say that I had a personal relationship with God and did not have real assurance that my sins were forgiven. After a student service in St. Peter's Church, Vere Street, led by the Rev. George Duncan, in the second term of my second year I heard the following verse from the Bible explained. 'Behold, I stand at the door and knock; if anyone hears my voice and opens the door, I will come in to him and eat with him, and he with me.' (Revelation chapter 3, verse 20, RSV). At the end of the service I asked Jesus to come into my heart and be my Saviour and Lord. From that time I have known Him in a personal way. I linked in with the College Christian Union (CU) and we were almost immediately involved in planning the School of Pharmacy participation in a university wide student mission the following Autumn. The Hon. Reverend Roland Lamb was attached to the School of Pharmacy CU as our missioner and helped us with our planning. At the mission several School of Pharmacy students committed their lives to Christ and there was a real interest in Christian things among the students and staff of the school.

The Christian students met daily for prayer in a large broom cupboard before lectures commenced. Over the next year about one third of the school (30 students) had links with the CU and around 60 came to the open meetings. In January 1954 some of us attended a London Inter Faculty Christian Union conference. We all found it very helpful and during that conference a Bible verse in the letter of Paul to the Galatians, chapter 2 and verse 20, became of special significance to me. 'I have been crucified with Christ; it is no longer I who live, but Christ who lives in me; and the life that I now live in the flesh I live by faith in the Son of God, who loved me and gave himself for me.'(RSV). During that academic year (1953-54) I was Missionary Secretary to the CU and tried to have a missionary focus for prayer. First I wrote for missionary information from the Regions Beyond Missionary Union, but after waiting for a while but receiving no reply I contacted the China Inland Mission (CIM). That is where my interest in CIM began. This led eventually to Joan and I setting out by sea in October 1958, together with our son Peter who was 18 months old, for Thailand, to help at the Manorom Christian Hospital. In those days we spent about five months in Singapore. There received initial orientation to South East Asia, learned something of the workings of the CIM/ Overseas Missionary Fellowship (CIM/OMF) as it was then called, were given our country and work designations and had a very preliminary introduction to the language of our designated country. It was further impressed upon us that we were needed at Manorom as soon as possible and so our language learning was concertinered to the absolute minimum. After Singapore, where Paul our second son was born in less than ideal circumstances for both Joan and him, we travelled to Bangkok in March 1959 by sea. We stayed there about two days, just long enough to complete formalities, and then travelled by train with Em Fry, our senior missionary, to Lopburi. There was no language school, but we had all completed linguistic courses and were expected to be able to organise ourselves to study our appointed language using a native speaker of the language as our teacher/informant. The difference for our language learning period was that we had six weeks of such study instead of the usual one year which was the norm at that time. Then we were responsible for the day to day functioning of the hospital pharmacy. Since the hospital had more than 25 beds it was required by Thai law to have a Thai qualified pharmacist and so before long I was seeking to explore what registering as a Thai pharmacist involved. The obvious place to enquire was the only place where pharmacy was taught in Thailand at that time. That was at the Faculty of Pharmacy building on the Chulalongkorn University Campus, Bangkok. The Faculty of Pharmacy was at that time administratively a part of the Medical Sciences University but because of its location was always referred to as Chulalongkorn University. A few years later it was divided to form two faculties. One faculty is now part of Chulalongkorn University and the other is a part of Mahidol University. Both are very large faculties.

The main buildings on the Chulalongkorn campus were visually very striking with creamy white walls and beautiful high steeply pitched roofs covered with mainly orange and green tiling which glistened in the bright sunshine. These roofs were in fact very similar to the roofs of temple buildings. There were tree lined roads around the inside of the campus with a central grassed area, which included a soccer pitch. At the opposite side of the campus from the main buildings and just inside a large double gated entrance there was a fountain and artificial pool. The large double gates that led into that side of the campus near the strikingly attractive buildings usually stood open. God had spoken to us both, but first to Joan, through Revelation chapter 3 and verse 8. 'Behold, I have set before you an open door that no man can shut. I know your strength is small,…'(RSV). These university gates spoke to us of God's open door. I took a colour slide of the gates, with the beautiful buildings behind, and usually projected it when speaking at meetings on our first furlough to indicate the open door into Bangkok universities that we believed that God had opened before us.

Mrs. Chawee Bunnag was the head of the Department of Pharmacy and was very helpful and friendly when I called in and introduced myself. The original pharmacy teaching in Thailand had been influenced by Mr Hale, an Englishman, as long ago as the 1920s. Since the 1939-45 war the Americans had increased their influence considerably and the pharmacy course in Thailand was very much influenced by the courses taught in the American Colleges of Pharmacy. Mrs. Chawee herself had studied for a Masters degree in America. To be told that the Thai course was more similar to the American curriculum than the British curriculum was very useful information for me. I then knew that I needed to acquaint myself with the differences between the curriculum I had studied in London and the current American curriculum. I also obtained a copy of 'Pharmaceutical Jurisprudence' in the Thai language. This was one of the subjects that I would be examined in and for which there was no English translation. The legal language of this book meant that I had to study a whole range of vocabulary which would not be used in every day Thai, medical Thai, or religious Thai. I suppose it is fairly obvious that when one is working in another country it is most useful to learn the language of one's particular workplace. The Thai language used in the Royal Palace relating to royalty and royal matters is known as 'High Thai' and this language is also used for religious matters. This must be studied by missionaries but is unlikely to be studied by business people. Now it was important that I gained an understanding of some legal Thai which would not normally be studied by a missionary.

In the four years we worked at Manorom Christian Hospital we did not travel to Bangkok very often but whenever we did, such as when we passed through to go or come from holiday in Huahin, I would always visit the Faculty of Pharmacy. Not only did I get to know the lecturing staff but I also got to know a Christian student named Yothin. Through talking with him I heard that there were no meetings organised for Christian students on the campuses of the Bangkok universities. The Lord started to lay a burden on our hearts to do something about this and we shared it with other missionaries. Although all the missionaries we spoke to shared our concern about this lack of evangelical student Christian witness the general opinion was that such a witness would be impossible. First there were the political problems. I have already referred to the fact that Thailand was under marshal law when we first lived there and that it was the time of the Vietnam War. There was the fear of a communist takeover in Thailand. Public meetings of more than four people were banned on the university campuses. Secondly there were the mission problems. The CIM had always been an inland mission in China. When former CIM missionaries came to Thailand the initial idea was to work amongst Overseas Chinese living in up country Thailand. Thus the CIM became known as CIM/OMF and then in 1965 as OMF. The CIM/OMF had an arrangement with the missionary organisations already working in Thailand that we would go to areas where there had previously been no missionary work. The Central Area, the Tribal Area in the mountains of the North and the predominantly Muslim area in the South of Thailand were all such areas, but Bangkok was not. Furthermore we had been designated to the Central Thailand Medical Team and it was unheard of for a medically qualified missionary in the Medical Team to switch designation to the Evangelisation and Church Planting Team, never mind to something as specific as Student Work. Thirdly we were not typical student workers and no one, at first, could really see us in this specific role. However, quite early on in my time at Manorom I was seen to have a role working with young people and was appointed as one of the five member Central Thailand Youth Committee.

In October 1960 I took the Thai Pharmacy Registration Examination and was formally registered in December as a Thai Pharmacist with the Number 787. The following November I was formally invited by staff at the Faculty of Pharmacy, Chulalongkorn University to help with the First Refresher Course for Thai Hospital Pharmacists. At that time the flood waters at Manorom were still receding and I left Joan in charge of the move back to the pharmacy department from where it had been evacuated during the flood to our hospital flat.

At the refresher course I contributed several written papers in English, plus the translation into Thai of an article I had previously published in English. In addition I took part in a public discussion in Thai. The course lasted for one week. In our prayer letter of May 1962 we wrote. 'This course continued to develop several good contacts I had previously at the Pharmacy College. There is a great need for an IVF type of work amongst the students. At the Pharmacy College alone there would seem to be about 10 Christians, but there is no on campus organisation to encourage or coordinate their witness. The Lord has several times brought this need before us.' Sometime after the refresher course several of the lecturers at the Faculty of Pharmacy said to me in personal conversation that I should consider becoming a lecturer at the faculty. This gave us the idea that I might be able to combine lecturing with Christian student work. Nevertheless I did not feel qualified to lecture since I only had a Bachelor of Pharmacy degree and I thought that I should at least have an appropriate Master degree before I should consider lecturing.

CHAPTER 6

A TEST PRESCRIPTION

About a year before our furlough (now known as 'home assignment') was due, the Central Thailand Field Council started to consider whether they had any specific recommendations for our furlough other than being involved in general deputation work on behalf of the mission. When I was asked I said that I would like to have the opportunity for further study, possibly for a Master degree, so that I could return to be involved with lecturing and initiating an evangelical student work in Bangkok. The outcome of this was that in general the members of the field council were interested in and sympathetic to this request but they stipulated that certain conditions should first be met to persuade them that this was indeed the Lord's will for us. These were;

- there should be adequate cover for the pharmacy department at Manorom while we were away for an extended period of time,

- I should have a better than average proficiency in the Thai language, (Comment: neither of us had been able to give more than a small fraction of the prescribed time allocated for language study because we were committed to full time medical work),

- I should obtain a relevant higher degree while on furlough, (Comment: we agreed, but living in Central Thailand in the early 1960s was about five weeks travel from the UK, so it was difficult to impossible to hear about available scholarships to undertake a higher degree in time to make application),

- I would need to help look for another pharmacist to take my place permanently at Manorom,

- I should have a lecturing position offered to me by Chulalongkorn University, Faculty of Pharmacy, at the appropriate time.

We were so pleased to have a partial go ahead from the Field Council that we took their reply very positively and set out our prayer list to pray specifically that each item would be met. Looked at in the cool light of day and without the eye of faith this looked pretty stark. In fact it was another set of circumstances which might have been described as impossible. But Jesus said, 'What is impossible with men is possible with God.' (The Gospel according to Luke, chapter 18, verse 27, NIV).

The above points made by the Field Council

might be expressed in the form of a 'Prescription' as below:

THE TEST PRESCRIPTION

The Central Thailand Field Council OMF Superintendent's Office,
Lopburi, Thailand.

For the OMF Central Thailand Field Council.

Supply: An acceptable mixture containing the following ingredients:
- a pharmacist for Manorom for the period of further study,
- a demonstration of a good grasp of the Thai language,
- a relevant higher degree,
- a pharmacist for Manorom, after our move to Bangkok,
- a lecturing position at Chulalongkorn University.

Preparation: Through faith in God by prayer and diligence.

Instructions: To be taken as a single dose to assure the Field Council that M & J should proceed to lecturing and student work in Bangkok.

Prescribers: Dr. FC Maddox, Medical Superintendent, Manorom Christian Hospital, Chainat, Thailand.

Mr. C Faulkner, OMF Central Thailand Field
Superintendent, Lopburi, Thailand.

How were our prayers answered? The first point
in the prescription above was met when Clair
Williams, a pharmacist from Melbourne Australia,
agreed to return from retirement. Clair had worked
with Drs. Chris and Catherine Maddox in China and
also at Manorom for about three years before we
arrived in 1959. Apparently Clair had originally
agreed to work at Manorom for six months but actually stayed on longer when she heard that we were in
the pipeline and so that she could link up with us
when we arrived. This was the reason we had felt
that we were being hurried up at every stage of the
way in our application procedures to the mission.
Since Clair had already worked at Manorom several
of the missionaries and other staff at the hospital
knew her and they were very pleased at the thought
of her returning for a further period.

The second point was initially made possible in
a somewhat unexpected way. The subject of eye
preparations, in particular the contamination of
ophthalmic solutions, was one of the interests that I
gained from preparing for the registration examinations to become a qualified Thai pharmacist in 1960.
There were quite a few reports in the literature, of
the 1940s and 50s, of patients who having suffered
some trauma to their eyes, had been prescribed eye
drops and subsequently been found to have developed an infection which destroyed their eyesight, or
even caused the loss of an eye. This was due to the

unsuitable methods of preparation, design of containers, inadequate antimicrobial preservation of multiple dose formulations and unsatisfactory methods of use of ophthalmic solutions. The organism which was causing a particular problem in contaminating ophthalmic solutions and destroying eyes was *Pseudomonas aeruginosa*.

Joan and I used to discuss these problems together and Joan had an idea about container design which would allow the container to be autoclaved without the high temperature and pressure destroying the rubber teat of the eye dropper. We developed the idea and wrote a short article, together with diagrams, which on 27 May 1961 was published in the Pharmaceutical Journal (the journal of the Royal Pharmaceutical Society of Great Britain). I later found that a Danish manufacturer had made commercial use of our design! But more to the point for us at that time, Professor D.A.Norton (Dan), Head of the School of Pharmacy, Bristol College of Science and Technology (which became the University of Bath in about 1966) wrote us to say that he had an interest in eye drop container design and that he found our article very interesting. He went on to say that if I was ever interested in doing further work in this area he might be able to offer me a Research Assistantship (RA) to work with him. We could hardly believe it, but I wrote back to say that if I could have the RA to work for a higher degree then I would be interested. His reply was that this position was not intended for the holder to work for a higher degree but to assist him with research. I replied that I would only be interested in the position if it allowed me to work for a higher degree, but I would try, in addition to undertake work for him related to eye drop containers. (This was done in collaboration with Mr. George Fletcher who was also offered an RA at Bristol. The specifications for the British Standard Eye Drop Container were based on our work.) Subsequently I was offered the RA position and I accepted it with a start date of 2 January 1963. The RA remuneration was probably intended for a single person who was a recent graduate, but it paid more than the ordinary studentship. This was welcome because we now had three children. Ann had been born in Manorom in August 1960. Nevertheless, later on, lecturing staff in Bristol expressed surprise that we could all exist on the RA income.

The plan was that we set out on furlough from Manorom in October 1962. Several months before that time I went to Bangkok to take the Fourth Section Thai language examination as set by OMF in Thailand. The result was quite surprising. I was awarded a mark of 90 % and was told that it was the highest mark given so far for that examination. The examiners told me that on that performance I would be able to pass the Fifth and final Section examination without further study. Although I did not test their prediction it meant that in their opinion my language was at the same standard as someone completing all the formal language examinations. Back at Manorom a few days later Dr. Catherine Maddox asked me sympathetically how the exam had gone. I said, 'Very well. Howard Hatton told me it was the best mark they had awarded in the Fourth Section Examination.' Catherine who was normally not given to banter, but knew that I could joke a little said, 'Pull the other one!' I didn't press the point. However, we were encouraged that the third requirement had now been met and in a very convincing and objective way.

In October we left the hospital with our luggage, by rowing boat, as the hospital was flooded for the third time in the four rainy seasons we had been there. When in Bangkok I visited the Faculty of Pharmacy and gave Dean Chalor a copy of the Manorom Christian Hospital Formulary 1962, which we had just completed a little while before leaving Manorom. The Thai Government Hospital Formulary was produced a little while afterwards but I do not know if there was any connection with our one. Clair Williams seemed to think that there might have been. Dean Chalor and some of his senior staff were very friendly and took us out for a meal before we left.

For the journey to Singapore we were given rather good berths on a Norwegian freighter, the Toledo, which had delivered its cargo to Bangkok, but had collected no return cargo, and so was sitting rather higher than normal out of the water. This was a cause for concern when we moved out into the Gulf of Thailand on 24 October and were hit by a very strong Typhoon which was reported to be 300 kilometers in diameter. That is about ten times the size that would be commonly expected. I read in a recent Bangkok Post article of Friday 20 December 2002 that this Typhoon was the cause of Thailand's biggest ever natural disaster. Many boats sank and hundreds of people were killed along the Thai coastal strip down to Malaysia. The newspaper article reported that nearly 1,000 people were killed in nine provinces. The bow of our boat would rise, juddering, high out of the water, lifted by the large waves and then crash back down into the water as the wave passed. There was some fear that the boat might have its hull structurally damaged. Joan was in a cabin, with Peter and Ann, and I was in a cabin with Paul. We had to strap ourselves onto the bunks with broad leather straps. That journey could well have been our last and the Captain was very pleased to be able to chart a course eastwards away from the worst of the storm. Interestingly, we received a letter after arriving home from Miss Audrey Hammond who prayed for us regularly. Audrey wrote that she read about the awful storm and worked out from our last prayer letter that we would be on the sea at the time of the storm and so she made it a matter of much prayer for us. We are grateful to a prayer answering God. (One thing we have been greatly blessed with over the years has been a group of faithful prayer supporters. Many are now in heaven, but a good number still pray for us. They continue to commit us, the work we are doing and the situations and people we are involved with, to the Lord. 'The prayer of a righteous man has great power in its effects.' James, 5: 16 (RSV). Not only missionaries and ministers but all Christians need prayer support in order to be effective in God's service.)

Arriving at Singapore the boat moored well out to sea and we had to climb down a metal retractable stairway on the outside of the hull. When on a little platform at the foot of the stairs we had to time our step across the gap into a small harbour motorboat rising and falling in the swell by about three feet from below the step to three feet above the step. The children were transferred to the small boat over the shoulders of seamen like sacks of potatoes, but Joan had to make the decision herself when to jump across the heaving gap, with a little help from a firm hand.

In Singapore we had to wait three weeks for our boat, the Fair Sky, which was making its passage from Australia to Southampton. This gave me the time to make the most of the good library facilities at the University of Singapore where we had a friend, Mr. James Hannam, who lectured in the School of Pharmacy. James was an Indian Christian Singaporean who had studied for his London BPharm degree while in his forties.

Daphne Parker, who had travelled to Singapore with us in 1958, was returning from the Philippines and we were very pleased to have her travel with us on the Fair Sky. Daphne was a children's nanny before joining OMF. While we were travelling home the Cuba Missile Crisis came and went. Joan had her birthday on board, about the time we left after calling in at Colombo, and we arrived at Southampton in the early morning of my birthday. It was a frosty morning and we did not have suitable clothing. Nevertheless we were kept waiting on the open quayside for what seemed to be a very long time before we eventually passed through the customs sheds and then onto a train, which was standing room only, through the hoar frost covered countryside to Waterloo. There we were met by mother and a next door neighbour from Morton. I was given an old ARP Warden's coat, belonging to my father, to wear. While staying at the CIM HQ in Newington Green I bought an old ford prefect car from a dealer recommended, I believe, by David Ellis. Then after Christmas in Derbyshire it was through the snow down to Bristol to stay in the basement flat of a Christian doctor and his family who lived above us. The car was left parked outside the house in the snow for many days after that. The accommodation had kindly been arranged for us by Mr. Charles Orton, the honorary CIM West Country Regional Secretary. The Reverend Peter Dawes, who was our minister when we lived in Crouch End, while I did National Service, also welcomed us. He was then a lecturer at the Clifton Theological College. We took leave of absence from the CIM/OMF from the end of December for the duration of my studies. The College pay cheque did not fall due until the end of the month, but our accommodation rental of £28 was due on the first of the month. No one knew that this left us with hardly any money, but 'Angels' posted more than £60 through our letter box in that first month. Getting Peter started at school, me organised for work and the family settled into the accommodation was quite a struggle. The heating and hot water arrangements were unsatisfactory, and we had to spread our day clothes on our beds at night to keep warm. That was a particularly bad winter and there was snow on the ground in Bristol for a total of 40 days. While we were in Bristol we attended the Alma Road Brethren Assembly, where George Muller had been a member in earlier times. At that time many medical people, such as Professor Melville Capper and Dr. David Cunningham, were members. One of the younger members, Mr. Alec Luff, had popped a leaflet, with details of the services and an invitation to attend, through our door. He was delighted with the response. The fellowship at Alma Road was a great blessing to us and was a great help in keeping us pointed back to Thailand. We also had some contact with Redland Parish Church where Charles Orton was a Lay Reader.

The old premises of the George Muller Orphanage, on Ashley Down, were now the premises of the Bristol College of Science and Technology where I worked. I felt very privileged and encouraged to be associated with the buildings which such a great man of faith as George Muller had made so famous in his days in Bristol.

It was hoped that I would register for an MPharm by research as an external student of the University of London and in February I made a visit to London to discuss how I could go about this. Working as an external student was not the best way to undertake a higher degree by research. There were many difficulties to be worked through, but eventually I was able to register for an MPharm, and then later to transfer the registration to that for a PhD. Then at a later date, I provided a supporting statement and filled in the appropriate forms to apply for a remission of time, so that I could submit my thesis before the normal registration period of four years for an external PhD had elapsed. This was successful. The title of my research was; 'Investigations of the resistance of *Pseudomonas aeruginosa* to chemical antibacterial agents.' It proved to be a very timely field of investigation and there has been continuing worldwide interest in this organism, particularly in medical situations, right up to the present day. At the beginning of the 1960s most of the research that was being done in the field of Pharmaceutical Microbiology in the UK was concerned, either with the activity of phenols against strains of the much used laboratory test bacteria *Escherichia coli*, or with the resistance of bacterial spores to heat treatment. My work provided an alternative field of clinically relevant research using a test organism which was causing many problems in medical and pharmaceutical practice.

Dr. Mike Brown joined the staff at Bristol a year or so after me and was a great source of help and advice to me for my research although for undisclosed reasons he was not allowed to be an official supervisor. In effect I was working without official supervision.

I spoke at the 1963 CIM/OMF annual Conference at Swanwick in the Easter break and after that at the conference at Llandrindod Wells. A pharmacist, Shirley Crook, was at the Swanwick Conference, and I understand she deliberately avoided me, so that she could determine from the Lord whether she should apply to OMF or not without being unduly influenced or pressurised by me! In the following November at another conference I believe we met both, Shirley Crook and Maelynn Adamson, who was also a pharmacist. Both eventually applied to OMF and were accepted for service in Thailand. We were very encouraged as we saw God's hand at work. All the ingredients which were necessary to dispense the 'Test Prescription' and, which would open the way for us to go to Bangkok for student work, were being brought together nicely and quite obviously not by ourselves.

In February 1965 we wrote our Prayer Circular Letter No.16 and I would like to quote a part of it to give a flavour of how we were feeling at that time.

'Imagine some pot-holers, who have been in the darkness of some deep underground tunnel, making their way back to the surface. Suddenly they notice a faint glimmer of light which grows in intensity as they struggle upwards. They are not at the surface yet, but their spirits rise within them as they clamber towards their goal. This is something of our experience. For a long time we have been busily, laboriously, sometimes faintly, struggling down in the depths. Now we have seen the first glimmer of light shining backwards through time from 27 September, 1965. This is the date we are booked to leave for Singapore on the good ship Chusan! (*We actually sailed on the Arcadia on 22 September*). The way is still difficult, there is much climbing still to be done, but our spirits have soared within us as we have seen the dawn break on what we trust will be the year of our return to the field.

The children will be returning with us, but Peter and Paul will go straight to Chefoo School in Malaya. Peter will return to Preparatory School in England at 9½ years, that is the Summer of 1966 and Paul will follow two years later (all DV). This path which leads to the parting of our ways from the children is not an easy one to tread, but we do it gladly in expression of our love for Him who took a path of much greater suffering for our blessing. We look to Him to provide the grace for us all to follow in His train.

Last November we had the joy of getting to know Shirley Crook and Maelynn Adamson who are both pharmacists and have offered to work with OMF. They will be sailing to Singapore this April (DV)'.

In May we heard from Mr Cyril Faulkner, OMF Superintendent, Central Thailand, that the plan for our return would be that we went to Manorom Hospital for a few weeks to help there and then moved down to our own house in Bangkok for the beginning of December. It was suggested that beginning early in January 1966 I should have a term of language study at the Union Language Centre, Bangkok.

CHAPTER 7

OPPOSITION

After two and a half years working long hours on my research I went to The School of Pharmacy, the University of London, in Brunswick Square in May 1965 for my oral examination. I made a phone call, from a phone box across the road from the School of Pharmacy, to the CIM HQ asking for prayer. They were actually in the middle of a prayer meeting at that time so I am sure that they prayed for me almost straight away. I was pleased that I had done this, because as I walked into the room for my examination, Professor Archie Cook was sitting in a chair waving in his hand a copy of my thesis towards an open window just behind his right shoulder. He said, 'I'm not going to accept this. It can go out of the window.' Such behaviour was totally unacceptable, but I don't think it was typical of Professor Cook's personality and was more likely caused by the stress of an illness he was suffering. If I had crumbled before such an outburst I'm pretty convinced that he would have thrown the thesis out, but not out of the window! His intention was to fail me and he worked at that throughout the afternoon. All I can say is that the Lord sustained me. For three hours Professor Cook and to a much less extent Dr. Chris Bean, his fellow examiner, grilled me with no let up. I can remember a cup of tea being put in front of me at one stage, but I never had the chance to touch it. One of the arguments put forward was that the work was not all my own and that other people must have done some of the experimental work. It seemed to anger him to a state of unreasonableness that I had completed so much research in so short a time. It was the 'red rag to a bull' syndrome. This was accentuated because his students were taking much longer to complete their PhD degrees. He told me of one lecturer who had taken 10 years to complete his PhD in microbiology. In fact I had developed, and statistically validated, rapid methods of investigation and I could probably obtain the equivalent data in one day that would take three or four days to obtain by the conventional run of the mill techniques. Then he challenged the statistical methods I had used, which were unknown to him, and which he did not understand. This was because I had worked with a biological statistician to develop from basics the statistical validation for the investigational method I had used. In the oral we had wide ranging discussions about microbiological methods of investigation and various key publications. He finished up by saying rather exasperatedly, 'Well you know your microbiology anyway.' At the end of the oral I was asked to rewrite the 'Introduction' to my thesis and include in a more prominent position the name of the statistician who had advised on my statistics. This request was very different from Professor Cook's original remarks, that he was not going to accept the thesis, and indicated how far the situation had been turned around during the course of the oral. My bound Thesis then had to be split open and the new 'Introduction' typed and included in a new binding. Of course all the page numbers also had to be adjusted and the internal references to pages within the thesis, so it was not a small amount of work. Unfortunately the binding was the expensive part, but it was all completed within six weeks and sent back to London University.

Dr. Mike Brown, who had been a great support to me throughout this time, was quite keen that I should stay on at Bristol because lectureships were becoming available to facilitate the transition of the college to university status. Bristol College of Advanced Science and Technology was soon to become the University of Bath and move to a new campus on Claverton Down. Dr. Dai Davies, who had just joined the staff, after completing his PhD at the University of Manchester, said to me in his forthright but basically kindly way, 'You are a fool going out to Thailand and not accepting a position here. I guarantee that within six months you'll be crawling back on your hands and knees asking for a job!'

By the time I had sent my revised thesis off to

London University it was then getting on towards August. We were due to move up to CIM/OMF HQ in Newington Green, London, by the middle of August to have inoculations and make other preparations for going to Thailand. I wanted to know if I would be needed for another PhD oral examination, because I was hoping to return to Thailand by boat at the end of September and the passages would soon need to be confirmed. The secretariat of London University could not give me an answer at that time, so we decided to proceed with our plans to return to Thailand and again travelled via Singapore. In Singapore, Joan and the two girls had the trauma of saying goodbye to the two boys (Peter 8 and Paul 6). All bore up nobly in accordance with what was thought to be expected of each one at that time. I then travelled with Peter and Paul by overnight train to Kuala Lumpur and then on by road to the mission school in the mountain jungle. This was called Chefoo School, and was situated in the Cameron Highlands, West Malaysia. The name Chefoo was the name of the equivalent CIM School of former years in Chefoo, China. The school was located in a very beautiful area but I had little time to explore that. Although everything was very new to them both Peter and Paul faced up to their new school very bravely and positively and the next day when I said my 'good byes' they were already settling in. I left feeling somewhat bereft because I was so used to having the boys around. After returning to Singapore to join up with Joan, Ann and Rose, Rose had been born in Bristol in August 1964, we travelled by a smallish Ben Line boat to Bangkok. A day or two after arriving at the Mission Home at the end of October, the Central Thailand Field Superintendent, Mr. Cyril Faulkner, visited Bangkok. He spoke to us in his quiet friendly and chatty way, more or less as we were passing each other in the lounge, saying, 'It looks as though you might not be doing student work after all, because it appears that you are still needed at Manorom.' This was a considerable shock to us and we expressed that we were not happy with this decision, which seemed to go against everything that we had been experiencing of the Lord's leading over the last three years. It was decided that we should go up to Manorom as soon as possible, work at the hospital for the month of November, as previously agreed, and discuss the matter of what happened after that with Dr. Christopher Maddox, the Medical Superintendent. Mr. George Williamson, an OMF Director based in Singapore with responsibility at that time for Thailand, also came to Manorom to help with the discussions.

The following decisions were agreed and I quote the Memo of 30 November 1965.

'1. It was agreed that Mr. and Mrs. Richards would reside in Bangkok for future student work in that city, especially among pharmacy students.

2. The move would take effect in December 1965, in consultation with the Field Superintendent regarding housing and in view of the family being settled in Bangkok for the

children's Christmas holidays.

3. Mr. Richards would study for one term in U.L.C., Bangkok, at his own expense.

4. During this term Mr. Richards will seek possible invitations for a part or full-time lectureship in the Pharmacy Department of the University. Future housing will depend on further investigations and developments as to the most suitable location, rental price etc., and in consultation with the Field Superintendent and Headquarters in Singapore.

5. After removal to Bangkok, Mr. Richards will be willing to help Manorom Hospital in cases of emergency, e.g. illness of Pharmacist of more than a few days duration, or the withdrawal of the present pharmacist earlier than anticipated.

(Various scenarios were then given but in effect did not apply because Clair Williams stayed on at Manorom for another year.)

Mr. Richards is willing to be responsible for official forms if difficulties arise in continuing the system which has worked satisfactorily for the last three years in respect of Manorom Hospital.

6. Mr. and Mrs. Richards will be regarded as medical workers on loan to the general work, and their work in Bangkok will be under the Field Superintendent. In cases of need the return of loan may be requested and discussed

with the Field Superintendent.

This does not preclude direct contact between medical workers and Mr. and Mrs. Richards for discussion of the work, nor preclude short visits to Manorom as may be conveniently arranged without interference to the Bangkok work.'

We were pleased to have all this dealt with 'officially' and put in writing so that we all had something to which we could refer if the need arose.

While in Manorom we heard that Joan's father had died. More pressure on Joan. Towards the end of the month, before the discussions with Mr. Williamson, we also heard that I had been awarded a PhD in Medicine, Non Clinical, by the Senate of the University of London. This latter news was, not only good news for us, it was also an essential ingredient needed to provide the complete mixture of conditions, set by the Central Thailand Field Council, to assure us all that it was God's will for us to move to Bangkok. Although I had not yet received a formal invitation to lecture in the Faculty of Pharmacy, I had received unofficial encouragements from lecturers at the university that such an invitation would be forthcoming. In the Thai way of doing things this meant that the decision had really been taken and would subsequently be processed more formally. Further encouragement was given by Professor Fairbairn, who had taught us at the School of Pharmacy, University of London, and who had visited the Faculty of Pharmacy in Bangkok a few months previously and had subsequently written to Dean Chalor strongly supporting my potential usefulness as a lecturer. So in effect the 'Test Prescription' was complete in every detail and the way it had all come together, despite opposition, gave us a great sense of knowing that God had arranged it all.

At the beginning of December we returned to Bangkok back on track with our original agreed plan of work. We were now under pressure to get a house set up in order to receive the boys who were due home from school about 10 days before Christmas. That was something to look forward to. It was also hard work because we had no servant help.

By this time we were both fairly exhausted both mentally and physically. We had been on the move and under a whole series of pressures for several months. During our last summer in England we forewent a holiday in order to make the deadline for catching the boat to Singapore and so to Thailand. We felt that if we did not make it at that time then we never would, particularly as Joan was expecting our fifth child in February and needed to get something approaching a settled existence.

There was yet another 'attack' on our getting started into the student work. A week or two after the boys had returned to Chefoo some kittens were left outside our gate and the girls adopted them as soon as they saw them. Because of the heat the girls would play in the 'garden' area wearing just shorts and flip flops on their feet. As the result they got scratched on their bodies and arms by the kittens, especially Rose who was the younger one. Then the kittens died. We were told by our landlady that on previous occasions people had abandoned their sick pets in the slightly quieter and less used road outside our house. Very concerned we took Ann and Rose to the Bangkok Christian Hospital and the doctor confirmed our worst fears that there was a real possibility the kittens might have had rabies. This is endemic in Thailand and one cannot take chances with this disease because by the time the symptoms appear it is too late to treat. It is 100 % fatal. Rabies anti-serum was injected around the scratch marks, mostly on Rose. This provided some immediate active protection but could not be relied upon to be effective as a treatment on its own. A course of rabies vaccine was also required. For Rose this was an injection a day for at least 15 days. Ann had less, I had less again and Joan had the least. Dr. Rachel Hillier (then Rachel Anstead) was doing language study in Bangkok at that time and kindly came round to give the injections. Getting to know Rachel better through this daily contact was a real pleasure. The vaccine had been prepared using duck egg protein. After about 10 injections Rose produced an allergic response to the injection and her face was puffing up. However, it was felt that the injections should continue and so she was also given a daily antihistamine injection to reduce the allergic reaction. Poor Rose! Rose was always very stoical, and she put up bravely with all of this, but the result was that she had an 'enduring' expression on her face and lost her cheerfulness, to a large extent, for a year or so after that. In the long term she also has had a tendency to have an allergy to some other things and we wonder if this was as the result of this episode. The important thing was, and is, that no serious symptoms of rabies developed and that was a great cause of relief for us. Again we had experienced God's overruling and protection in these traumatic events and we were very thankful and encouraged.

It needs to be said at this stage that in general we did not cope well with the spiritual attacks and stresses and strains that we faced seeking to start a new work in Bangkok and having to try and work through problems and difficulties pretty much on our own. Life for Joan was very lonely, spending most of her time in the home with no natural contacts. It was also a very limited environment for the children at home, who would quickly get bored, and we faced constant strain from being concerned about the children away at school. Life was physically hard trying to keep up with our programme, live within our means (trying to live as near as possible to the living allowance for upcountry missionaries, which was impossible), constant noise even at night with nightclubs nearby, and of course no air conditioning, to help combat the heat, which now has become the norm for many. I could not understand why we kept facing one crisis after another. Having seemingly overcome one crisis I thought that if we were seeking to do the Lord's will and live in obedience to Him we would then proceed smoothly seeing the Lord overcoming all the obstacles with no need for a great struggle or a great battle to be engaged in on our part. Such personal battles seemed to indicate personal failure. We knew that there was a battle to be fought with spiritual weapons in order to advance the Lord's kingdom but we did not understand that there would be a need to constantly battle with problems in our own lives. Those we consulted were not able to give us a great deal of help other than to perhaps seek ways of avoiding some of the problems by being less submerged in the work. This could be said to be a bit of an escapist approach and not a direct answer to the problem. Although I do accept that rest and relaxation are very helpful and should be incorporated into one's life where possible. Nevertheless in the type of situation in which we lived at that time such options were extremely limited, apart from an annual holiday and an occasional visit for a meal to the OMF Bangkok Mission Home. It has to be said that this was not encouraged as it was really intended for people visiting Bangkok from upcountry for business or passing through for holiday or furlough. Victorious Christian living had more to it than we or the ones we consulted could explain. They would as likely as not soon turn from our questions and take the opportunity to share their own problems with us, which was friendly, but did not lead to any practical answers. We were in great need of the teaching we later received from the Rev. William Still in Aberdeen (1986-1996). That is that Christians have an enemy, the Devil, who constantly seeks to cause them problems and make them ineffective in God's service. All the Christian's problems are not of his own making. Those that are he should be able to identify and deal with by confession, repentance and seeking to go on in God's strength. However, there will be many problems that are not directly attributable to the Christian. These are likely to be attacks from the Devil, or his agents, and should be recognised as such and fought, through prayer, seeking God's specific help to defeat the Devil, and by active obedience to the teaching of God's word the Bible. Therefore, we should expect problems as the norm for the Christian and not be disheartened by them because we see them as our personal failure. Rather, we can even see them in a positive way, in that the things we are doing are attracting opposition, because in fact they are having positive effects in advancing the Lord's purposes. I hope this aside in order to state an important spiritual truth will be helpful to someone or other who may be facing discouragement in the Lord's service. Think of the teaching of the book of Job and of the constant opposition our Lord faced, not only through the temptations of the Devil in person in the wilderness, but also throughout His whole ministry. Remember, through the cross and resurrection the Lord Jesus defeated Sin, Death and the Devil.

With regard to the above discussion it should also be noted that, especially when seeking guidance to a particular way forward, the Christian may be confused as to whether a particular obstacle is of the Lord or of the Devil. In that situation pray, 'Lord if it is of You, enable me to accept it, but if it is of the

Devil, enable me to resist it, in Your Name. Amen'.

(This is similar to the prayer recommended for praying in such circumstances by the well known missionary of the China Inland Mission, Fraser of Lisuland.)

CHAPTER 8

ENCOURAGEMENTS

Early in the New Year we had the great encouragement that I was invited to a meeting of the Christian Pharmacy students and asked to take on the role as formal advisor to the group. They had been meeting every month throughout the current academic year with Suttida a fifth year pharmacy student as their leader. There were about 10 students at the meeting, mostly from the third to fifth year of the pharmacy degree course, but there was also a younger student, Somgiat, who was a cousin of Suttida. I think he was in his first or second year. The interesting thing about Somgiat is that soon after completing his pharmacy degree he undertook further training for the Christian ministry and became pastor of a Pentecostal Church in Bangkok.

I also made contact with Dean Chalor and Mrs. Chawee at the Pharmacy Faculty and was invited to give two lectures to fifth year students. Two senior staff also listened to the lectures and afterwards confirmed that they would like to invite me to be a Special Lecturer beginning at the start of the next academic year in June. Our vision was being realised. We had obtained the openings we had prayed, trusted and worked for. Now we would be able to start with an evangelical student witness in the Faculty of Pharmacy and hopefully expand that witness to other faculties. Our overall plan was for the Christian pharmacy students to get established as a group in the first year and form a core group for wider evangelism, such as giving out tracts at functions where students gathered in large numbers, and for evangelistic meetings to which students from other Faculties would be invited. Then in the second year we were looking to the Lord to help us start another cell group in a second faculty. There were about 50,000 university students in Bangkok at that time of which perhaps 10-15,000 were at Chulalongkorn University and a similar number at Thamasart University, the other big university. Both were prestigious universities, but especially Chulalongkorn, and the students had quite a status in Thai society of those days and were given considerable respect. The students themselves could be rather proud of their position and some maybe were even a little arrogant.

I was also able to enrol at the Union Language Center for one term, January-March. This would be a great help in brushing up my language after three years away. Shirley and Maelynn had arrived in

Bangkok and were also involved in language study. Claire Williams was happy to stay at Manorom until Shirley was ready to move there at the end of the year.

Our Prayer Circular Letter No. 17 of 22 January 1966 contained the following:

'We need an ever increasing volume of praise and prayer that the yet precarious beach-head into University Student work may be expanded, in spite of all the opposition, into an effective advance.

"…a wide door for effective work has opened to me (*us*), and there are many adversaries." The first letter of Paul to the Corinthians chapter 16, verse 9, RSV.

Please pray:
1) to keep the "wide door" open
2) to make our work "effective work" and
3) to overcome the "adversaries".'

When the new academic year started in June I started lecturing and the pharmacy cell group began meeting weckly for Bible study, prayer and fellowship over the first five month semester. In those first days we used Scripture Union Bible study outlines in Thai, but we did not necessarily stick to the same method all of the time. All of the students who met and studied together like this found that it was very worthwhile and were enthusiastic. It was just what they needed, and probably had not experienced before, and it was possible to see some of them making rapid growth in their faith and Christian understanding. There were many things that needed to be considered in order to best fit in with the commitments of the students and the best time and place to meet. The average attendance was about 50 % of the maximum possible and we only attracted one non Christian. But we did have separate evangelistic meetings which were attended by about 60 different students from various faculties. A start had been made and the general pattern had been set.

In fact, one could say that two starts had been made, because I had also been asked to teach the Bible in Thai three times a week, at a Chinese Christian high school, within walking distance of our home. In effect it was a Church School for ethnic Chinese families who spoke a minority Chinese dialect in Thailand. But of course all the students spoke Thai. The person who had previously done this teaching had left and I was asked to take their place at least for the first term. This was a far better use of my time than I had first thought. My class consisted of 34 boys and girls in the 13-15 year old age bracket. After overcoming some initial discipline problems with two or three of the boys we settled down well together. I was left to choose what I taught and I tried to show them linkages between the teaching contained in certain passages in the Gospel of John and teaching in parts of the Old Testament. For example, I might get them to look at John, 3:14-15 (RSV). 'And as Moses lifted up the serpent in the wilderness, so must the Son of Man be lifted up, that whoever believes in him may have eternal life.' Then this was compared with, Numbers, 21:8-9 (RSV). 'And the LORD said to Moses, "Make a fiery serpent and set it on a pole;

and every one who is bitten, when he sees it, shall live." So Moses made a bronze serpent, and set it on a pole; and if a serpent bit any man, he would look at the bronze serpent and live.' Then I would give them the opportunity to draw a picture to illustrate the incident that we had read about. There were some very talented artists among them. I would also set them a set of short answer questions on the passage and discuss their answers, to try and make sure they had understood what it was all about.

My class was so encouraging I asked if I could have a special meeting for the older pupils in a large hall. This was agreed and I took the opportunity to preach the Gospel. At the end of my message I asked those who wanted to commit their lives to Christ and to receive Him as their Lord and Saviour to come forward. It was fairly unusual to make an appeal like that in Thailand at that time and I myself had not done it before. A whole lot of pupils came to the front, so I thought they must have misunderstood what I had said, so I sent them back to their seats and explained again that it was only those who were going to make a real commitment who should come forward. Twenty nine of them came forward the second time. I prayed with them and arranged to have some special Bible classes for these and other Christians at the school who wanted to come along.

Seventeen years later Joan and I attended an International Fellowship of Evangelical Students (IFES) East Asia Regional Conference in Nakhorn Phathum, Thailand. The Chairman of the Board of Thai Christian Students (TCS) came up to me and said, 'I was one of those students who came forward when you made the appeal at my school.' I heard later that the second General Secretary of TCS, Mr. Tonglaw, was also a pupil at the school at that time, but I didn't know him, and I don't know if he attended any of my classes.

After one term I arranged with another missionary who was working in Bangkok to take the class, but I have often wondered whether I made the wrong decision. It is hard to have a correct perspective when just starting into several things at once and perhaps I was too wary of being diverted from the university students. I also had responsibilities as chairman of the Central Thailand Youth Committee. Theoretically a whole variety of people could have access to high schools but an effective entry to the university scene was much more difficult to obtain. We had to be single minded in seeking to achieve what we believed the Lord had set us apart to do.

Mr. David Adeney and Mrs. Adeney visited and stayed with us for a day or two during our first few months in Bangkok. They were once CIM missionaries in China but now David was Eat Asia Regional Secretary for IFES based in Hong Kong. David recommended that we should consider producing some of our own literature for widespread free distribution. He also recommended that we should include an address, so that interested enquirers could contact us and, that we should offer opportunities for group Bible study to university students and a free Bible correspondence course for those who were interested. Our target was to distribute the tract at the time of the Asian Games which were to be held in Bangkok 9-20 December 1966.

We planned to make it a joint project with the Christian students and to have the theme 'So run that you may obtain' or as it was finally called 'Run to win'. The front would have a picture of the Thai National Marathon winner for 1996 who was a Christian. We also planned to write asking Christian student movements in the other 15 countries in Asia which were taking part in the games if they could supply testimonies from Christian athletes.

Prayer Circular Letter No.19 of February 1967 gave an account of what happened.

'We would like to begin this letter by bringing you up to date with the Asian Games Tract Project. When last we wrote we were hoping to obtain testimonies from Christian athletes taking part in the games. Letters were written to Christian student organisations in nine of the countries due to send athletes to Bangkok. Only three replies eventually reached us and no testimonies were forthcoming from any athletes, not even from our Thai Marathon runner whose photograph was being used as the cover of the tract.

Time was getting short so Joan went ahead with writing the tract, which after many discussions, including help by the students, was eventually ready for print. Further minor obstacles were overcome and by the end of November the first tracts were ready and, just the day before the Games were due to begin the final consignment arrived from the printers, making 30,000 in all.

During this time, despite no appeal for money, but in answer to prayer, money started coming in to pay for the tract and just the right amount arrived for us to pay the bill of almost £50. This money came from Malaysia, England and various sources in Bangkok including the students themselves. In this way the Lord greatly encouraged us by confirming that He was with the project,

Prasart, the President of the Pharmacy Students Christian Fellowship, organised the distribution by transferring many of the tracts to his digs, so that there would be a tract supply right near the National Stadium where we planned our major distribution. Most of the tracts were given out during the first weekend of the Games with the help of other Christian friends. The students met together for a time of prayer each time before going off to give the tracts to spectators leaving the various events. On the Saturday a group were out from 3.30-11.30 pm. An encouraging by-product of working together on a project like this was the unifying and deepening spiritual effect on each member of the group involved.

Sixty one replied to the tract. Twenty two were in the age group 11-16 years; 27 were in the age group 17-25 years; 6 were over 25 years and 6 were university students. Thirty two of these 61 replies requested to do group Bible study in addition to the Bible Correspondence Course. We are not certain yet whether this can be arranged or not, but we are certainly going to try and get the university students into group bible study with other students. Prasart wrote to the four university students who had replied by Christmas time and invited them to join the Christmas programme planned by the Pharmacy Students Christian Fellowship. All four students turned up and one brought a friend.

These results cause us to rejoice and believe that God is doing much more than we can actually see at present. We with the Pharmacy Students Christian Fellowship greatly value your prayers, especially for next (academic) year's programme and for the tract follow up responsibilities.'

I would like to include here thumb nail sketches of some of that first group of Christian students in the hope that it gives you a feel for the developing situation and the spiritual battles we still had to fight. Here is how we described them, in confidence, to selected praying friends, at the beginning of February 1967. That is, as we approached the end of our first academic year together.

'Ampiga is a fifth and final year student from a Bangkok Chinese Christian family having two sisters and one brother. Her father died last April, on the day Ampiga, Mattana and I were due to go to a Christian student conference in Malaya, causing us to cancel the trip. Ampiga attends a Chinese speaking Church and is active in their youth group. This last year Ampiga has been Treasurer of the Pharmacy Students Christian Fellowship and in addition to a pleasant personality and bright Christian testimony she is a good pianist. Pray that she may successfully qualify as a pharmacist and know the Lord's leading in the future.'

'Mattana is a fifth year student from a Thai

Christian family having two younger brothers. Her father is a lecturer in the Southern Baptist Bible College here in Bangkok and Mattana is a member of one of the Southern Baptist Churches. Mattana has been Secretary of the Christian Fellowship this year and has a good testimony, but seems to become easily discouraged. Pray that the Lord will enable her in the final examinations and guide her very clearly as to the next step.'

'Prasart is a fourth year student from a Chinese Christian family in South Thailand having two older brothers, one a lawyer and the other a medical student. Prasart has a strong Christian witness and is very active in Christian work. Pray that the Lord will further equip and enable Prasart so that he will be greatly used in Christ's service. Prasart has been President of the Student Christian Fellowship and he has also been one of the three elected student leaders for the fourth year students (120 of them). Prasart is also the leader of the Thai section of a recently formed Christian and Missionary Alliance Evangelical Church in Bangkok. The Fourth Thai Church (Presbyterian) also consider him as the leader of their young people. Next year's pharmacy committee has not yet been elected but Prasart would again seem to be the Lord's man for the job. Pray that he may do well in his studies despite all of his extra responsibilities.'

'Yenjai is a third year student and one of nine children of a Bangkok Chinese Christian family having Christians going back five generations. Yenjai is a member of the same church as Ampiga, and is also musical but rather shy. When she attends Bible studies she is usually a blessing but we would like to see much more of her.'

'Ampurwan is a third year student and another one whose origins can be traced back to China. We have not had much opportunity of getting to know Ampurwan but we feel that she is not very strong in her Christian life and therefore in need of our prayers. We are not sure of her church connection.'

'Wirode is a third year student of Chinese ancestry whose home is about 40 miles west of Bangkok. He is very shy but would seem to have grown considerably as a Christian this year. Goes home every other weekend, but when in Bangkok comes to the student Bible studies.'

'Wanchai is another third year student from a Chinese family living in Bangkok. We do not see much of Wanchai but he seems to have been helped when he has come along. He was very keen to give out our special tract at the Asian Games. We are not sure of his church connection.'

'Buntida was converted as a student but is still rather a weak Christian. She has only twice attended the student meetings and needs much prayer for her examinations, especially as she has failed once.'

In case you are wondering why no first or second year students are mentioned it is because for the first two years all medical, dental, laboratory technician and pharmacy students study together in another place.

Our next confidential Prayer Companions Letter was number 20 and was sent out in May and provides an update on the above.

'Ampiga, Mattana and Buntida, mentioned in our last letter, all passed their final examinations. Mattana came among the top few and was awarded special honours. Ampiga and Mattana both have good jobs, but Buntida is not yet happily settled. Prasart unfortunately failed one examination and is re-taking it this week. We pray that he will be enabled to pass it and not have to repeat his fourth year.

The committee for the Pharmacy Students Christian Fellowship for 1967-68 is as follows: Prasart, chairman; Wirode, secretary and Yenjai, treasurer. Decisions about where and when to meet this year and plans to reach other students have yet to be made.

A Dental student has contacted me about Bible studies in the Dental Faculty and there are plans to ask permission to have a weekly meeting within the Dental Faculty. This prospect thrills us. Let us continue to pray.

Ampiga is attempting to get some Christian graduates to form a Graduates Fellowship. This development could, under God, mean so much for other graduates, local churches and the establishment of a Thai run student work.

We are still praying that the contact with Thammasart University students will develop to the place where a Student Christian Fellowship will be formed there.'

In answer to prayer progress was being made in the ways along which we had prayed for and one might gain the impression that everything was fine.

On the personal level we were finding it very difficult. Living in Bangkok was quite different from
living in Manorom. The cost of living was very low
in Manorom, when we lived there, although the
living was fairly basic. The rent of our house was
almost just a token at 100 Baht a month. This was
especially so as it had no facilities such as running
water, electricity or toilet and the building itself was
in a rather dilapidated state. It was also supposedly
haunted and no Thai would live there at the time
when we took it on. Nevertheless, when some work
was done on it to provide toilet facilities, and to fit
simple ceilings below the corrugated iron roof, to
help protect against the oven like heat, it became
home to us and we were very happy living there. In
addition there were several other missionary households connected with the hospital and so there was a
mutual information and support system in place.
The hospital was greatly appreciated and the local
inhabitants were very friendly. The situation in
Bangkok was very different. The Vietnam War was
in progress and Bangkok was used as a place for
'rest and recreation' by thousands of US troops.
Renting a property to Americans, or other foreigners, was a prime source of income for Bangkokians.
The rental for our house was 40 times our Manorom
house rental. The Bangkok Sports Club was next to
us on one side of the house and the car park came to
within about four feet of our house wall. Some of
the club members would stay comparatively late
and make a lot of noise talking and shouting to each
other as they left from the car park. On the other

side was a house similar to ours and at first occu-pied by another missionary family, but they moved away within a few months of our arriving. The members of a band from the Philippines then rented the house. The band who played at a night club also arrived back late with accompanying noise. They would sleep late in the morning and then after lunch would have about two hours practice. On the other side of their house and very close to it was a Japanese night club called the 'Ginza'. Taxis would bring and collect clients frequenting the nightclub until the early hours. One way and another it was difficult to get sufficient uninterrupted rest. We also found it very difficult to get suitable help in the home. Our first experience was fairly disastrous. The lady was not only expensive but a poor cook and dishonest. We found that she passed things over the fence to a friend in the car park. Quite a clever trick, another one had, was to break the contents of eggs into a plastic bag and then conceal the bag and contents by hanging the bag from her belt inside her long Thai style skirt. She would leave the broken egg shells on view in the kitchen to show that she had used them in our food. When questioned about certain ingredients such as onion, that could not be tasted or seen in the food she would say that they must have dissolved while being cooked. Mrs. Hong (Swan) a Christian lady who was the wife of the caretaker of the Fourth Thai Church which was just across and a little way up the road from us took pity on us and came and helped for a while. Mrs. Swan was a good cook and very pleasant and was someone Joan could have Christian fellowship with, but she could not read or write, so everything had to be remembered. Unfortunately she could not stay with us long because she had five children of her own and she was really too busy with her own family. Patin who had worked for us in Manorom, and who was a favourite of the family came to work for us for about 14 months. It was very good of her, because Bangkok was very strange to her, but she made a big difference to our comfort and we were very thankful. Patin left us in December 1968 because she was needed back home to help with the rice harvest. This inevitably meant that a heavier load again fell onto Joan.

There was also the spiritual warfare involved in any work of God and perhaps especially in a pioneer work. In those days we had no OMF fellow workers undertaking church planting type work in Bangkok who might face similar type situations to ourselves. However, there was a weekly Prayer Meeting which new workers undertaking language study, OMF Publishers staff, Mission Home and OMF Regional Office staff would attend. We also found having young children away at school very difficult and we possibly made an unnecessary rod for our backs in trying to write each of the children two short letters a week instead of the one letter required. Not too hard a task when there was just one away at school but quite demanding when there were three of them. Peter at age nine had gone back to England to preparatory school in August 1966. Just a few weeks before that Ann, not quite six years old, had gone off with Paul, seven, to Cheefoo. We were not too good at sharing these problems but the Prayer Companions Letter No. 20 of 10 May 1967, already referred to above, does make an attempt to do so. I quote from that letter again below.

'Greetings from Bangkok, where the Hot Season is just giving way to the Wet Season (still hot!). We have found the hot season very tiring and a heat wave at the end of April just about flattened us. Bangkok is witnessing a building boom and many tall concrete buildings are mushrooming all over the city. It is said that the increased amount of concrete surfaces in the city is making the city more uncomfortable to live in because of all the heat reflected by these surfaces.

Rose at 3¾ years is full of bounce and her energy so shatters us that we find ourselves gasping for her bed time. Our limited environment means that Joan has to bear the brunt of her momentum, although I was forcefully introduced to it when Joan did two weeks full time language study recently. Megan, 15 months, has been walking since February and is a little 'pickle' and full of mischief. Despite the wear and tear we wouldn't be without them and they are a great joy.

We have good news from the children at school, Peter, 10 years (England), Paul 8 years and Ann 6 years (Malaya). Their being away keeps us busy writing letters and keeping abreast with their developments. *The separation involved has caused many heartaches and it is only as we look to the Lord continually, both for the children and for ourselves, that we can keep going. The Lord continues to encourage us that we are in the place of His appointment but this subject has caused us to waver more than once.* Peter is due to fly out to us in July, together with Joan's Mum, arriving on the 13 July. This gives him just over a week with Ann and Paul before they return to Chefoo. Peter will return to England the beginning of September and Joan's Mum will return at the beginning of August.

The verse 'My grace is sufficient for you, for my power is made perfect in weakness.' 2 Corinthians 12:9 (RSV) is a great comfort.'

The italics were not in the original. I can remember repeating to myself many times during the time in Bangkok 'Though he slay me yet will I trust in him' Job chapter 13 verse 15, Authorised Version of the Bible. At times it seemed to be as bad as that.

Joan wrote in a similar vein 10 months later in Prayer Circular Letter No. 20. 'There is so much more I would love to share with you individually but time would fail to tell of all the joys and sorrows, of our struggles, our encouragements and discouragements, how sometimes we feel it is the most wonderful thing on earth to be here doing student work, and how other times we feel we cannot go on any longer and we haven't even the strength to pack up and go home! How we value your prayers for us and for our Thai friends for whom the spiritual battle is even fiercer.'

However there were some encouragements which showed us how the Lord was working in a far wider circle than Bangkok. I received a letter from

Theodore Welch, who with his wife Pam, was preparing to leave England with the OMF. Theodore's parents spent their lives working with CIM and his father was Deputation Secretary in England when we were in the process of joining the mission. We had got to know Theodore a little when we had contacts with the CIM HQ at Newington Green. Theodore and Pam were due to travel by boat to Singapore sometime in March. In Singapore they would, in consultation with Directors of OMF, agree their designation to a particular country and sphere of work. Theodore was a surgeon and was interested in having a university position where he could lecture and support Christian witness. He wrote in general terms but we could see that here was the possibility of someone else coming to Thailand, to do something similar to what we were doing, but probably in a different university. In the middle of February I wrote what I intended to be a generally encouraging reply to Theodore to try and inform and not to pre-empt his designation discussions in Singapore. To have people like Theodore and Pam join us was in line with the vision the Lord had given us for the expansion of the student work and encouraged us in our praying.

In May 1967 we read in a Newsletter from the OMF British Home Director, Mr. Scott, that he had read in a letter from Mr. Arnold Lea, an OMF Director in Singapore, that Mr. Andrew Way, a new worker at the Orientation Centre in Singapore had a 'distinct burden for university students'. I immediately wrote to Andrew to introduce ourselves and to give him an up to date picture of what was happening in Bangkok. Andrew was an electrical engineer and I was able to tell him that we already knew a keen and influential Christian student, Suwatt, who was studying for a degree in electrical engineering at Chulalongkorn University. I also told him that three Christian students in the Dental Faculty were in the process of asking permission from their Dean to have a Bible study within the faculty each Saturday afternoon.

During this student vacation Prasart called around to visit us at our home on several occasions and in conversation expressed the desire of wanting to know the Lord in a deeper way and be more useful in His service. He also borrowed one or two of our books to read. His life was a great challenge and encouragement to us. He also used to visit Mr. and Mrs. Martin, who worked at the Christian and Missionary Alliance (CMA) Office, about five minutes walk away and helped lead a Thai service on Sunday with them.

An English service was held at the CMA compound under the leadership of Mr. Bill Carson and we used to attend this service with our children. Bill and Delores Wilson who worked at OMF Publishers also attended with their two children. This service eventually developed into the International Church which met at the Rama Hotel during our time in Bangkok. After a year or two Bill Nabors, a former CMA missionary in Thailand, returned to be the first full time minister. I was one of the Board Members of this church in its infancy. For many years now it has had its own

Church building and it has become a well established church in another part of Bangkok where
many of the international community live.

CHAPTER 9

TRAGEDY AND GROWTH

The academic year had just got under way when one morning I saw Bill Carson walking down our path with a very distraught look on his face. My heart sank and I thought that there must have been some tragedy. He brought the sad news that Prasart, together with his mother, had been killed in a traffic accident. On 2 June, Prasart had been driving to Korat in the north east of the country and I understand that the car he was driving had been in collision with a big truck. This was devastating news for us all. We felt that we had lost a family member and others felt the same.

The funeral service was held on 4 June in the Second Thai Church. Prasart had just entered his fifth and final year and just about all of his 120 classmates were present at the service, including one senior member of the Pharmacy Faculty staff, Dr.

Wichien. I was asked to be one of the main speakers and to speak of Prasart as someone who had been one of his lecturers. Of course we had a much closer relationship than that and I believe that I was specially enabled to be able to speak factually about Prasart and his life and witness in such a way that also made the Gospel clear to his fellow students.

On the day of Prasart's funeral, Wirode became President of the Pharmacy Students Christian Fellowship (PSCF). Wanpen, a fifth year female student who had become a Christian mainly through Prasart's witness in the previous year was baptised on 2 July and became Secretary of the PSCF on 9 July. Bible studies were held weekly in our home at 2.00 pm on Sunday, followed by open prayer and fellowship. Two Fact and Faith films, 'Windows of the soul' and 'Facts of faith' were shown in the Faculty of Pharmacy with official permission. We also showed slides of a pharmacy student outing, which had been organised by the faculty, as an item of general interest to encourage as many students as possible to come along. During June-August we held regular meetings for graduates and took a group to hear Mr. Oswald Sanders, General Director of OMF speak at a special evangelistic meeting held in the grounds of the CMA property.

The Dental Students Bible Study started on 17 June and was held with official permission in the entrance reception area of the Ladies Hall of Residence within the Dental Faculty. This meeting was held weekly at 1.00 pm on Saturday. Mr. Lim, a fourth year student was the leader of the group together with two Christian fourth year students, Sirirat and Dusadee (ladies). Up to seven students who were interested to know more about the Gospel attended these meetings, as did Andrew Way, once he was settled into language school. This was how Andrew received some first hand experience of what was happening in the student work. He was a great help and encouragement and we saw him as the Lord's provision for the work. There was a year's full time language study to complete before he could have a greater involvement and then Andrew wanted to have experience of up country Thailand and work among young people in that situation. For these reasons, when he left language school in Bangkok, he spent a period of time at Manorom where there were many young people associated with the hospital. He then returned to Bangkok to be the key OMF person associated with the Bangkok student work after we returned to England in July 1969.

Dusadee was the younger sister of Yothin who was so vital in being part of the original vision for the evangelical student work. Dusadee became a lecturer in the Dental Faculty of Chiang Mai University and became well known as a Christian there.

It was encouraging that the dental group had obtained permission to meet on campus because that was also one of the things we had hoped from the beginning might be possible. The pharmacy group had asked permission to use a room in the faculty building, but there were many demands on the existing accommodation and they were not given permission. However, they did meet quite regularly at one time outside the front of the building in a shady area where there were some fixed tables and bench seats. During that time Mr. Eustace Govan, who was OMF East of Scotland Secretary living in Edinburgh, visited Bangkok. Eustace was making a tour observing examples of the work of OMF in SE Asia and Japan. He attended one of these pharmacy open air cell group meetings and an evangelistic student meeting in our home. Many years later he told me that those student meetings were the highlight of his whole trip.

October and November were quite active months and there were some important policy decisions made during that time. We arranged an interfaculty meting on 14 October to which seven pharmacy, eight dental and seven Thammasart students came along. After a time of singing, I gave a talk on 'Life with a purpose', and this was followed with refreshments. You will remember that Thammasart was another large university. It was famous for Law and Political Science and we were seeking ways of helping to establish a Christian student witness there. On 29 October we had a visit from Mr. Chua Wee Hian who was in the process of taking over from David Adeney as East Asia IFES General Secretary. On the afternoon of Sunday 29 October we had what we called an Interfaculty and Schools meeting to which we aimed to have key leaders present to meet with Wee Hian. By this time Joan was having weekly meetings with a mixed High School group.

Wirode, Yenjai, Wanpen and Preecha represented Pharmacy , Lim was the Dental group representative.

Thamrong was there from Thammasart, Suwatt from Engineering (Chulalongkorn), Pitoon from Science (Chulalongkorn) and Ampiga represented the Graduates. Ten high school students also attended. Suwatt led the singing, I spoke on the first chapter of I Thessalonians, reports together with slides of the pharmacy and dental groups were presented by Wirode and Lim respectively. Ampiga gave her testimony and Wee Hian gave an illustrated talk on the work of IFES in Asia which Lim translated into Thai. This gave the students a first hand introduction to IFES, which we had told them about previously and planned that they would eventually link up with.

At that meeting we could also report that we were in the process of producing 10,000 copies of a chapter from Billy Graham's latest book 'World Aflame'. The chapter was 'The Inescapable Christ'. We had called the booklet 'No Escape' and it was being produced using Thai on one page and English on the facing page. It was intended that at least 5,000 of these booklets would be distributed at the annual Thammasart-Chulalongkorn football match, which was played in the National Stadium during December, with many thousands of students from both universities attending. Again there was a tear out slip that could be used to contact us by those interested in further Bible study. We were also producing 15,000 more copies of 'Run to Win' for distribution at the South East Asia and Philippines (SEAP) Games to be held in Bangkok 9-16 December.

In the evening Wee Hian, Joan and I had a meeting for fellowship and to discuss the future of the

student work. Wee Hian made the following suggestions and offers of help.

1. We should write to David Michelle in Japan
asking about the availability of a Bible
Correspondence Course that could be used
for the follow-up of the tract.
2. The Fellowship of Evangelical Students
Malaya would pay for one person to represent
the student work in Thailand at a conference
in Singapore.
3. IFES would pay for one person to go as a
Thai delegate to the conference in Japan
planned for August 1968.
4. It was suggested that six Malaysian students
visit Bangkok, at their own expense, at the
end of March to be boarded with Christian
families and to attend a Thai student houseparty.
5. IFES would help with the support of a Thai
Staff worker. It was suggested that such a
person should first attend the Discipleship
Training Course being set up by David
Adeney.

It was also understood that we would be made
IFES Associate Staff, but that this would be first
checked out with Mr. Cyril Faulkner, OMF Central
Thailand Field Superintendent.

We all felt that the Lord had blessed our time
together and we were pleased to have been able to
identify together some pointers to guide us in the

way the work could be developed in the future. The next special item on our programme was a graduate and student houseparty to be held at Manorom on 11-12 November.

It was good to be able to have some of those involved in the student work interact with some of the medical team in this way and show that they were not mutually exclusive areas of work. We also appreciated having Drs. Chris Maddox, John Hay and John Townsend together with Mr. Arporn, the hospital business manager, contribute to the programme. There were eleven students, eight from pharmacy, Lim and Sirirat from dentistry, Suwatt engineering and two graduates, Ampiga and Ankana. Together with four missionaries, plus Rose and Megan, we made 19 in all and we set out together on the Saturday morning by the 7.00 am train from Bangkok to Takli. After getting off the train and a 30 mile bus journey we arrived at the Manorom Guest House about 1.00 pm for lunch. In the afternoon we had a meeting at which we considered 'Leading a group Bible study', followed by a tour of the hospital and talks from Dr. Chris and Mr. Arporn. The students and two graduates were shared around three hospital households for the evening meal. In the evening we had lots of singing and testimonies from John Hay and John Townsend followed by a message from Pastor Toyotome, a Japanese pastor, who was visiting the hospital. Lim translated.

Andrew Way and Ann Goodall, who were both doing full time language study were able to accompany us for the weekend away. It is interesting that

Ann ended up doing student work in South Thailand – so another missionary had been encouraged in the right direction! Another subsequent development was that Wanpen became the first Thai pharmacist to take charge of the Pharmacy Department at Manorom Christian Hospital. Later she married Graham Seed an OMF missionary from New Zealand and became an OMF missionary. The student work thus was a direct benefit to the medical work. The encouraging thing is that many of the students involved with student cell groups ended up as key members of their churches and not a few became ministers of churches. In fact the general level of education of Thai ministers/pastors was influenced in a positive way by the student work. Few if any evangelical pastors had degrees when we first went to Thailand in 1959. In about 2000 we met Dr. Henry Bridenthal, OMF, in the Bangkok OMF home. Henry was the key person in initiating and establishing the higher level Bible College in Bangkok, known as the Bangkok Bible College (BBC). He told me that in his opinion it would not have been possible to start the higher level Bible College when they did if the student work had not been functioning and providing a source of motivated Christian graduates. Conversely, of course, the BBC met a need in providing a convenient means for Christian graduates to undertake degree level Biblical studies without having to go overseas.

On the Sunday morning we joined in the service at Manorom Church and after lunch returned to Bangkok having had a very enjoyable and spiritually profitable time away together.

The 11 day visit of seven Christian students from Singapore, which included a three day seaside camp at Huahin with eight Christian university students from Bangkok went well. The need for daily personal Bible study was recognised by some to be something that they should be aiming for if they were to grow in spiritual maturity. A need for a better understanding of spoken English was also felt by the Thai students and so in the long vacation after the camp we organised Bible Discussion groups in English twice a week.

The needs of the 200,000 high school students were also exercising our thoughts and prayers. We were praying that others would see this great need and be called to this work. We were also aware that the needs of students in Thamasart University were not being met and we were seeing the need for a dedicated office to help with the organisation of the growing work. More literature for thinking non Christians was also needed. We were considering producing another booklet in Thai and English using another chapter from 'World Aflame.'

The teaching and research that I was involved with also kept me on my toes. Soon after starting at the Faculty of Pharmacy I said that I would like to do some research. Quite surprisingly at that time, 1966, very little if any research was being undertaken in the School of Pharmacy. A very friendly lecturer, Miss Nuanjira, who had completed a Masters degree of London University, told me that I should prepare a research proposal and submit it to

The Thai College of Surgeons to request for funding. It was the time of the Vietnam War and I put forward a proposal to undertake research in the provision of creams for the treatment of burn wound infections. No reply was received and I thought that the proposal had been turned down. Then one day, about a year later, Nuanjira came round to our house and she said;

'I've got good news for you. Your proposal for research funding which you sent to the Thai College of Surgeons has been successful and you can now start on the research work.'

I replied, 'Oh, I had forgotten about that. I'm now too busy and I don't have time to do research. Please tell them I don't want to accept the grant.'

'You can't say no!' I was told in no uncertain terms. Arrangements were made for me to carry out the research at the Thai Armed Forces Pharmaceuticals Factory. My boss in that situation was Colonel Prasert, a very friendly Thai Army Colonel, who was a pharmacist.

There was a newly built three storey research building in the grounds of the factory that had not yet been used. I was given the whole of the middle floor of that building plus three Research Assistants. These consisted of an officer from each of the three armed forces. All were qualified pharmacists but none had any research experience. A driver from the pharmaceutical factory collected me from my home and delivered me back again at least twice a week. We obtained the equipment and materials that were needed for the research project and worked together for about six months. A publication in an international journal resulted but I cannot be sure if any final product was actually used in the clinical situation. There were often communication gaps as to what went on 'down the line', so to speak. In my experience I have often been left not knowing the actual details surrounding the outcome resulting from a particular situation that I have had a part in. I once heard, in another situation and some time after the event that someone had presented at a conference, research results from my investigations which I had recorded in an internal report.

In June 1968 four non Christian high school students started studying the Bible with Joan on Saturday afternoons. In addition a Christian high school student started weekly Bible studies for a group of his non Christian friends. They met on a football pitch between 7.00-8.00 am before the start of classes. During August three engineering students started weekly Bible study and fellowship meetings on Chulalongkorn University campus with Suwatt as the leader. Also in August Lim had attended the IFES Conference in Japan as the Thai delegate. Then in November a group of pre-medical students started Bible study and fellowship meetings in the pre-medical school.

A central committee was then formed consisting of representatives from the Pharmacy, Dental and Engineering Fellowships. A constitution was drawn up based on that of the UK Inter Varsity Fellowship of that time. We called the combined fellowship groups, Glum Kristian Mahawithyalai (GKM) –

University Christian Groups. (This name was changed, by the Christian students' central committee after a training camp in 1971, to the more appropriate name of Nagsygsa Kristian Thai, or in English, Thai Christian Students (TCS). The new name identified the organisation as being Thai, which was and is very important, and it seamlessly covered all students whether they were studying at university or not. The central committee of 1971 was very influential and was composed of students who remained key people from then onwards in the future development of TCS. Krassanai, a dental student who had been greatly helped by Andrew, was the chairman, Tonglor, an engineering student was the secretary and Wimonsee, an accountancy student, who was led to the Lord by Dorothy Mainhood at one of the special student meetings in 1969, was the treasurer. Wimonsee, later married Samuel Lee who also became a key person in the work of TCS.)

Theodore and Pam Welch were in Bangkok for language study by this time and very encouragingly were given the go ahead to proceed to Chiang Mai to undertake lecturing and student work after their time in Bangkok was completed.

The Lord was working in many ways and in many situations. By the time our furlough was due in August 1969 Andrew Way had returned to Bangkok from his time of up-country experience and took over the responsibility for the ongoing work with students from us. We could leave knowing that Andrew would seek to progress the work towards the goal of an evangelical student work linked to IFES and fully under Thai leadership as the Lord continued to guide and provide.

It is quite encouraging to compare one of our prayer letters written early in 1966 with a prayer letter written in September 1969. I wrote the following in Prayer Companions Letter No.18 on 14th February, 1966.

"To reach 50,000 university students with the Gospel is not going to be accomplished in an afternoon. Frankly it is an impossible task but with God all things are possible. Paul accepted the challenge of the 'Macedonian Call' of God to Evangelise Europe. We accept the challenge of the 'Bangkok Call' of God to evangelise the university students; and that 'we' definitely includes 'you'.

The task is great, the time is short and the workers are few therefore every move must be an effective move towards the accomplishment of our goal. We therefore stand in great need of God's wisdom and discernment. It was the enormity of the task that caused Solomon to request 'Give thy servant therefore an understanding mind to govern thy people….' 1 Kings 3:9a. Revised Standard Version. We need that 'understanding mind' to pray and work aright. We need that 'understanding mind' to be able to pick out God's leaders in this student world and train and encourage them for all we are worth. We need that 'understanding mind' to be able by God's Holy Spirit to enthuse every Christian to be a witnessing, evangelising Christian."

"The School of Pharmacy is part of the University

of Medical Sciences consisting, in addition to Pharmacy, of a Pre-medical School, two Medical Schools, a Dental School and Nursing, Public Health, Medical Technology, Tropical Medicine and Medical Science Schools. Key contacts into each of these faculties need to be prayed for and established. Likewise into the other five universities of Bangkok; Chulalongkorn, Thammasart, Fine Arts, Agricultural and Educational. Not to mention a big Technical College and also the Graduate world. The key is Christian students to head up the work in each of these places. Also let us right from the beginning ask God to raise up Thai graduates who will hear His call and be enabled by Him to be trained for full time work among this vast student population.

Another priority is that we will be able to organise our own leadership training conference as soon as possible."

Many of the things prayed for in 1966 were already a reality in 1969, as is seen from the contents of part of Prayer Circular Letter No.22 of September 1969.

"The student work in Bangkok has been handed over very smoothly to Andrew Way, (OMF missionary from England). Andrew is also helped in the work by several other OMF missionaries.

The Thai University Students Evangelical Fellowship, (known as GKM) which we have been privileged to have a part in bringing into being is continuing to function and grow. Since February the GKM has had an office from which the work is coordinated. The rent for this office is at the present contributed by other Christian students in Asia through the International Fellowship of Evangelical Students (IFES).

The present academic year for Bangkok's five universities started at the end of May and there are Bible Study/Fellowship Groups functioning in several faculties. The Medical Science University, known as Mahidol University as from this year, has the following groups. Pharmacy/Dental combined, Pre-medical, and a group in the Sirirat Teaching Hospital. Dorothy Mainhood, (OMF missionary from America) is the advisor for the Pre-medical and Sirirat groups.

Chulalongkorn University has a new group in the Education Faculty. The Engineering Faculty group was to combine with the Science Faculty this year as numbers of active Christians are small, but so far this combined group has not functioned well. A combined group is just forming in the Commerce and Political Science Faculties and it is hoped to have a group in the Chulalongkorn Teaching Hospital. Then at the Asian Institute of Technology, where graduates from many Asian Universities come for post-graduate study there are several Christian students and for the last 18 months several of these students have met together regularly for Bible study and Fellowship.

Please pray for the Christians seeking to lead these groups as it is a very hard task with many discouragements. May the Christian students have a desire to meet together and may the Lord so bless them that they will be strengthened in their Christian lives and be enabled to reach out and influence other students for Christ.

There is a Central Committee which together with Andrew, coordinates and backs up the witness in the universities, this committee needs our prayer.

Bill Merry (OMF from America) has been teaching English at Thammasart University since June and we are trusting that he will soon be able to initiate the formation of one or more Bible study groups in that university. This Autumn, Theodore and Pamela Welch (OMF missionaries from England) will be seeking to initiate student work in Chiangmai University, North Thailand. Theodore is a surgeon and will be teaching surgery in the Medical Faculty.

Andrew is following up contacts in the Agricultural University with the purpose of exploring the possibility of students having their own Bible Study/Fellowship meetings.

Another encouragement is that a group is now regularly meeting in a Teachers Training College in Paknampho some 200 miles north of Bangkok. We have had contact with several students in Teachers Training Colleges in and around Bangkok. This is another area into which the work should expand.

The high school students of Bangkok numbering several hundred thousand are still largely un-reached with the Gospel. One fellow hearing of the university witness started a Bible study on the football pitch of his school about 7.00 am one week day, but several workers are needed in order to get a real witness to high school students started.

During December we trust that about 5000 copies of a new booklet produced for university students will be distributed and used of the Lord to set some on the path to knowing the Lord Jesus for themselves.

The crowning joy of our four years in university student work was when one of the 1968 Pharmacy Graduates, who had come to know the Lord as a fourth year student, became the first Thai Pharmacist to take charge of the Pharmacy at Manorom Christian Hospital – thus spearheading the way for having Thai Heads of Departments at Manorom."

Soon after we returned to England and were living in very fine temporary accommodation at Laleham, Middlesex, which members of All Saints Laleham church had prepared for us, Theodore Srinivasagam, from India, came to stay the weekend with us. Theodore was in the process of completing his PhD in marine biology at the University of Southampton and was very interested to meet with us in order to learn more about the student work in Thailand. We were very privileged to get to know Theodore at that time and it was a great encouragement to learn of another person who God was preparing to work among Thai students. When Theodore had completed his PhD he went to Thailand with OMF. After language study he obtained a lecturing position at the Agricultural University (Kasertsat University), on the outskirts of Bangkok, near Don Muang airport. There in coordination with Andrew Way he initiated a student Bible study fellowship linked in with the growing programme of witness to university students. This work continued to prosper under God's good hand through students themselves taking on a far greater responsibility for the work, initially under the leadership of Krassanai, and in collaboration with several OMF missionaries. In addition there were many additional influential ministries to follow, such as Ada Lum's Bible teaching ministry beginning in 1970, Prasarn's ministry as the first Thai staff worker beginning in 1972, Samuel Lee spearheading the High School Student work beginning in 1974 (Samuel a graduate engineer from Hong Kong had been converted in 1969 through the witness of Felix Liu, a very gifted Christian from Taiwan, while they were both post-graduate students at the Asian Institute of Technology), Tonglor's ministry as the first TCS general Secretary commencing in 1976 and also in the same year the commencing of the vital ministries of Makino and Isu Naoyuki, who were Japanese missionaries with OMF. Dentist Lim was the first chairman of the TCS Board. These and succeeding TCS staff workers, general secretaries, board members and student leaders all had their important parts to play and no attempt is made here to record all God's work in and through TCS in subsequent years. The purpose of this account, however, is solely to concentrate on the beginnings of the evangelical Christian student work in Bangkok and to give Glory to God for what He did in those early days.

PART III

MAHASARAKHAM 2

CHAPTER 10

TRAVELLING IN ISARN

Before returning to some more key developments involved in establishing the Faculty of Pharmacy and Health Sciences I would like to mention some of the other aspects of our lives in Mahasarakham, which were important in our day to day living, and had a considerable influence on our lives. For example, travelling daily by car was both a challenge and a form of education for me. Exploring the area in which we lived provided us both with a very interesting and enjoyable method of relaxation. The education I obtained was in the intricacies of driving Thai style! I will share with you some of my insights and experiences in driving and touring. You might even find that knowing something about driving in Thailand will be helpful to you one day!

The vast majority of drivers in Thailand, of whatever vehicle, have not received any formal instruction on how to drive. In recent years a theoretical driving test has been introduced but there is no practical driving test. As a result many drivers do not have the basic skills of driving. Not many people that I know change down a gear when entering a corner. Even though speed is lost in the corner most will just labour the engine until it picks up speed again on leaving the corner. Should the speed drop so much that, not only does the engine make sounds of labouring but the gear stick also starts to judder, then a change down is made. Starting on an incline, using a release of the handbrake, as the clutch is let out and the gear engaged while accelerating slowly is not something I have seen a Thai driver perform. A little roll backwards before engaging the gear to stop the roll and gradually accelerating away is the accepted procedure. I was once given a lift by a driver who said that they had never used the reverse gear and always avoided situations where reversing might be necessary. On another occasion I was driven about two miles on busy roads used by fast traffic by someone who never changed gear upwards beyond second gear. When this second gear driver needed to stop, they first switched off the ignition and then put their foot on the brake. Fortunately I was able to avoid any further lifts from both of these drivers!

There is no such thing as an MOT reliability test for vehicles in Thailand and many are badly maintained. Tyres, particularly on trucks and country buses, may be badly worn so that no tread is visible. Various lights may no longer function as intended. It can give one quite a surprise at night on an unlit road to realise that the single light coming in the opposite direction is not a motorbike after all. One's intuition may fail to alert the senses, that the light in fact emanates from the headlight of a pick-up truck, until just before the dim shadowy outline looms into view and its nearside swishes past too close for comfort.

A general understanding of vehicle maintenance may also be lacking. There are adverts on Thai TV showing a driver unable to get his car started or to drive it up a slight hill. The situation is completely transformed by having the oil changed to the right brand of motor oil. This message obviously struck home to one of my support staff who often drove our faculty vehicle. When my car battery was flat one morning, I got the car started with the help of another lecturer who had a set of jump leads. I drove to the Faculty and asked the member of staff who often drove our faculty vehicle to take my car to a garage and get the battery charged. 'It doesn't need the battery charging,' he said, 'it needs a change of oil.' 'No it doesn't need a change of oil, please take it and have the battery charged.' Off he went to get this done and then parked the car near our accommodation. The next day the battery was flat again and I had to have help again to get it started. When I got to the office I found that my member of staff had not had the car battery charged but had taken the car for a change of oil. What can be said, except, 'now take the car and get the battery charged'.

Driving in Thailand is on the left hand side of the road. However, it is fair to say that rules of the road are open to wide interpretation. It is essential not to expect others to strictly observe rules or follow common courtesies. I have heard it said that when driving one has to try and be a mind reader and that is good advice in Thailand. Be prepared for anything and don't take your eyes of the road for a second would be my advice. Do not rely on having an automatic right of way. It is common for vehicles to come out from side turnings even when another vehicle is within a few yards of the turning. Large lorries will do this, presumably relying on the fact that they are just about invulnerable to damage from a car. Motorcycles also do this. They specialise in swerving out just a few feet in front of cars, either because they cannot control their bike, or they get a kick out of dicing with death, or they have a mistaken belief that they have some charmed existence. Sadly this is not backed up by the facts on road accidents. Another common driving trait is for the driver of a vehicle about to be overtaken to drift across the road to their right so that the passing driver can find they have run out of road. Increasing speed to prevent being overtaken is also common.

Vehicles may approach on the same side of the road that one is travelling along. Motorcycle riders would seem to do this as of right but they sometimes do run into danger. Drivers of cars and lorries do this when the road has a central reservation and they want to take a turning leading off the opposite side of the road to which they are on. They should drive past the turning and then take the next opening in the central reservation and make a 'U' turn back to their turn off. Instead they take the gap in the central reservation one before the desired side road and then drive in the opposite direction to oncoming traffic until they reach their turn off. 'U' turns are permitted in Thailand except when specifically prohibited with a sign. Roundabouts are few, so the 'U' turn is very common.

Another situation which is even more dangerous than that just described occurs when one drives on a road with just one lane in either direction. A driver may swing out to overtake when he does not have sufficient space to do so and then while driving on the wrong side of the road will flash his headlights at any oncoming traffic to indicate, 'get out of my way I'm coming through'. I must emphasise that flashing lights in Thailand means 'I'm coming, get out of my way.' Little imagination or thought is needed to realise that this is a dangerous manoeuvre, especially when it is a large vehicle. This is not uncommon when one bus is racing another to be first to the next pick up place.

One can assume, as a general rule, that a big vehicle will not give way to a smaller vehicle. But then motorcyclists do not seem to accept this. Children under ten may be seen riding motorcycles on busy roads, possibly carrying an even younger passenger. Parents seem not to do much to prevent this and may themselves provide very bad examples of dangerous riding habits. They quite commonly have two passengers and maybe three and these passengers are often small and vulnerable. It is common for a mother to ride pillion clutching a baby, just a few months old, on one arm and a whole lot of shopping, or other items in the other hand. Helmets are very rarely worn although they are required by law. Wing mirrors, front and back lights, or indicator lights are rarely all functioning on the same motorbike. I once mentioned to a friend that the thing that concerned me most when driving at night was the motorcyclists who had no lights functioning on their bikes. 'What motorcyclists with no lights?' she asked, 'I never see any'!!

Traffic lights are another source of potential danger. In the case where they are functioning in the normal way they may not be heeded by all drivers. A friend told me a joke about traffic lights. 'Green means go. Yellow means go faster. Red means go even faster!' The traffic lights may also just flash red or just flash yellow. Presumably this is so everyone can proceed with caution, but this does not appear to be obvious to all drivers. A difference from the UK is that drivers are, as a rule, allowed to turn left against a red light, as long as the way is clear. This is helpful in keeping traffic moving.

Another different custom in Thailand is the use of direction indicator lights. Winking right and left indicates that the driver intends to turn in the direction indicated. Flashing both lights means 'I'm coming straight on,' not, 'Warning I've got a problem.' A small branch of a bush or tree lying on the road means the same as a red triangle. That is 'You are approaching a hazard, such as a broken down vehicle'

To add to the above factors influencing the dangers of driving in Thailand is the whole issue of driving under the influence of either alcohol, or drugs, or both, which apparently is a major issue with over 20% of Thai drivers. This is undoubtedly a cause for much of the reckless and irrational driving that occurs and a reason why the road accident death rate rises at holiday times. The major Thai holiday occurs a day or two before and after April 13, which is the Thai New Year. It is known as the Songkran festival and many people return to their parent's home to pay their respects and to enjoy themselves. First I should give some background information about the Songkran festival before giving the downside of road accident statistics. Foreigners will know Songkran as the water throwing festival. Originally the water was poured over the hands of the parents and the parents blessed their children in return. It was a time for making merit by doing good, principally, but not exclusively by making gifts to Buddhist priests and temples. Doing good is a very deeply rooted concept in Buddhism and Thai society. Thais like to make merit as often as they can, and increasingly as they get older, because they believe that their status in their next reincarnated life depends on the amount their good deeds in this life counteract the influence of their bad deeds. Lecturers I was friendly with when I first had contact with Chulalongkorn University considered that I was accumulating a lot of merit for myself by working at Manorom Christian Hospital in up country Thailand instead of taking a lucrative job with some business in Bangkok. A Thai young man makes merit for his mother by going into the priesthood, a belief that ensures that nearly all Thai men spend at least a short time as a Buddhist priest. Making merit is also seen by some as a way to ensure that this present life works out well. A senior Thai politician, who was found guilty of financial irregularities and barred from taking part in politics for five years, concluded it was due to his bad luck (not misdeeds) and he must now spend time making merit to restore his good fortune and ensure that everything went well for him again.

In recent years the water throwing at the Songkran festival has become very excessive and can sometimes be antisocial, and even dangerous, with pressurised pumps being used to hit people with jets of water. Revelry associated with the holiday break has also become excessive and a lot of alcohol is consumed, especially by young people. Merit making is probably left to the older people. In the Songkran holiday of 2003, between 12 am on 11 April and 12 pm on 16 April, 594 people were killed through road accidents and 39,725 were injured. Roughly 80% of these were motorcyclists and 20 per cent were under 15 years old. Possibly as many as 90% of the motorcyclists did not wear helmets and 51,470 motorcycles were confiscated because the owners did not posses a driving licence. Many of these would be children and no doubt the motorcycles could be reclaimed after the festival was over. Of the motorists that were killed it would appear that 60% had been drinking alcohol and few were wearing seatbelts. These terrible figures were despite a determined government campaign to reduce accidents during Songkran 2003. It would be good advice to drive as little as possible during major public holidays!

When the whole problem of driving safety is considered there is a common thread running through the whole issue and that is a general lack of law enforcement. This is a great weakness in Thailand in every area of life. When at Chulalongkorn in the late 1960s Dean Chalor asked me what I would alter in the practice of pharmacy in Thailand if I had the opportunity. I said, 'I would enforce the law that pharmacists must be present in their pharmacies throughout the working day and not just in the evenings after they returned from their other job.' He said, 'I agree with you. Why don't you say that publicly?' I said, 'No. It would not be appropriate for me to say it. Why don't you say it?' We both laughed. The position is still the same today, almost forty years later.

I have mentioned that the government car that we were loaned was absolutely essential to enable us to function on the university campus and in and around Mahasarakham. It also gave us the possibility of exploring some parts of NE Thailand (Isarn) that were unknown to us. Mahasarakham province is located in the middle of the 19 Isarn provinces. This region has the largest population (over 20 million) and the greatest land area of Thailand's five geographical regions (North, Northeast, East, Central and South Thailand).

Isarn has a long international border with Laos along its northern and eastern boundaries. The River Khong (Mae Nam Khong in Thai), more often called the River Mekong in the UK and Western countries, rises in the Himalayas and enters the South China sea off southern Vietnam. On the way it flows through south west China, physically forms almost the entire border between Thailand and Laos and then flows on through Cambodia and across southern Vietnam.

Isarn has another international border, with Cambodia on its south east boundary. The north west of the NE Region also has provinces which are adjacent to the south east of the North region; a province in the south west bordering the Central region; and provinces in the south adjoining the north western part of the East region of Thailand. The only region of Thailand with which Isarn does not share a boundary is the Southern region.

Most of our car journeys were relatively short being about 100 – 150 miles, so it was inevitable that these journeys would be into neighbouring provinces to visit the provincial capitals of Roi Et, Kalasin and Khon Kaen. These capital cities have the same names as the respective provinces. Khon Kaen city is 50 miles from Mahasarakham town and was made the regional capital of Isarn when Field Marshall Sarit Thanarat was in power in the early 1960s. He was a native of Khon Kaen and that may have influenced his choice! At that time many people were surprised it was not another city such as Nakhorn Rajasima (Korat) or perhaps Udon Thani or Ubonrachathani. All of these had larger populations than Khon Kaen although the location of Ubonrachathani in the south east of Isarn would be a disadvantage. The other three cities, Korat, Khon Kaen and Udon are all on the one and only north-south railway line. At that time these cities were also on the only major road with a metalled surface (Friendship Highway – a joint Thai-US project) passing through the region and connecting Bangkok in the south with Nong Khai and the border with Laos in the north. Whatever the merits of the case Khon Kaen benefited greatly from Sarit's decision to make it regional capital and in particular from the related decision to locate the region's first university there. There is also another factor that we personally believe was an influence for good in the development of Khon Kaen, although some may raise their eyebrows! After visiting Khon Kaen in 1984 and Nanjing, in China, in 1983 we believed that God spoke to us through reading Acts chapter 19 verses 8-20. In those verses we saw how God worked in Ephesus. God gave us a burden for the peoples of Nanjing and Khon Kaen and the vision that He would do the same thing for them as He did, through the Apostle Paul, for the people of Ephesus. We wrote to the people who regularly prayed for us – our praying friends – and shared with them our thoughts and said that 'We are seeking to enlist 200 people who will pray regularly (daily if possible) for these two cities for three years. Therefore please take this as an invitation to you and to others you know who would like to be involved.' For our part we undertook to provide them relevant information and pointers for prayer by means of a special prayer letter, which replaced our previous prayer letters, and began with that letter of invitation in January 1985. It was called 'Strategic Prayer.' About twenty years later the facts are there for those with eyes to see and minds to understand. Both cities have grown in importance nationally, both pharmacy institutions have become very well known and influential nationally and internationally in Asia and both cities have a vibrant Christian community who have reached out and been a blessing to people in the towns and villages in their surrounding areas. I must resist getting too carried away about these events at this stage as 'The Tale of Two Cities' could form a book in itself. However, I give a few more details below!

Our connections with Khon Kaen developed from 1983 when I was asked by the British Council to act as their Consultant in providing advice to Khon Kaen University (KKU) to help with establishing their new Faculty of Pharmaceutical Sciences. My first visit in that capacity was made in 1984 and my collaboration with the university has been continuous since that time. During our time at Mahasarakham the Faculty of Pharmacy and Health Sciences benefited in receiving help and support from several of the lecturing staff based at Khon Kaen. Another benefit, which we personally received, resulted from our involvement with the Khon Kaen Chinese Church, which was founded in 1979. An interesting 'coincidence' of an experience I had when I first visited Nanjing occurred on my first visit to KKU. After I had been there a few days one of the staff took the opportunity, when no-one was near, to put their hand on my shoulder and whisper in my ear 'I'm a Christian too!' For some reason the unexpectedness of this made a shiver go down my spine! It was also on my first visit to KKU that I met and became friendly with Sataporn, a lecturer in the Faculty of Agriculture. He had become a Christian while studying for an MSc in Australia and he now acted as Advisor to the Thai Christian Student group at KKU, which became one of the most vital groups of Christian University students in all of the Thai universities. During the time I knew him at Khon Kaen, Sataporn was one of the most effective and influential Christians, not only in KKU, but also in Khon Kaen city. He was a great encouragement and blessing to me and created many opportunities for me. I remember well on one occasion when we were visiting the homes of university staff living on campus one of them asked him, 'Can you explain to me what the Mormons believe?' 'No, but I can explain to you what Jesus Christ has done for you.' was his reply and this he did. On another occasion a foreign academic had visited his faculty and Satarporn was concerned that he had not had a chance to share his faith with him. When it was time for the visitor to leave, Satarporn offered to carry his case so that he could walk along side him and discuss something that might be of spiritual benefit to him.

Kalasin is the neighbouring province to Mahasarakham to the north east and the town of Kalasin is only 20 miles from the town of Mahasarakham. In character it is very similar to Mahasarakham but in the Rim Pao Hotel Kalasin had an additional asset - quite a pleasant restaurant. We occasionally visited this if we were free on a

Saturday. Kalasin province has also become famous for the recent discovery of dinosaur remains when excavations were taking place near a temple. Most of the Isarn provinces are famous for the production of fine silk cloth and certain villages in Kalasin produce some especially highly sought after silk products. The provincial general hospital was also one of the hospitals where we were seeking to develop the pharmaceutical practice so that the hospital could be used as a suitable location for our student practice placements.

Roi Et province is to the south and east of Mahasarakham. The geographical locations of the two provincial capitals within their respective provinces are such that the town of Roi Et is, like Kalasin, only 20 miles or so from Mahasarakham. Features of Roi Et are a large lake in the centre of town which can be used for leisure activities and an exceptionally tall standing Buddha statue in the centre of the town. Our interest in Roi Et was much the same as for Kalasin – a hotel restaurant and a provincial general hospital. We also had a further interest develop there when one of our PharmD students, Mr. Teerawut, together with his pharmacist wife, developed a very good community pharmacy in the town centre.

We were interested in Nakhorn Phanom because the President of MSU had plans to establish a satellite campus there. It is one of the northernmost provinces of NE Thailand, on the east bank of the river Khong, as it flows seawards. Nakhorn Phanom was also where Ho Chi Min lived in exile from

Vietnam for many years. While living there for around 20 years he could be visited relatively easily by supporters from Vietnam which is only 30 miles or so away from Thailand at that point. This relative closeness of NE Thailand to Vietnam also made it very easy for communist infiltrators to enter Thailand in considerable numbers in the 1960s. The war in Vietnam would seem to have prevented the take over of Thailand by communism but for a while the Isarn region seemed very vulnerable. When we went to Thailand in 1959 it was being widely predicted that Thailand would be taken over by communists within 10 years. We were advised that we should be ready to move out within 48 hours leaving no evidence behind that might incriminate local Christians.

Nakhorn Phanom is about 140 miles north east from Mahasarakham. We planned to travel to Kalasin on Friday evening and stay overnight at the Rim Pao Hotel. Then we would continue our journey on Saturday arriving by midday so that we would be able to have a look around on the Saturday afternoon. There is a hotel on the river bank known as the Riverside Hotel, where university lecturers had told us they stayed when visiting Nakhorn Phanom, and we planned to stay there overnight and return home on Sunday. We wanted to complete all of our travel in daylight as there were potential hazards along the way and no such things as ambulances or call-out car breakdown services were available.

After leaving Kalasin town we headed for the district town of Somdet. From there the road snaked its way over a mountain range, covered with rain forest, and down into the provincial town of Sakon Nakon. On a previous occasion we had driven to Somdet but a problem had developed with the car air conditioning system such that the condensed water discharged into the passenger side foot well. Although we continued far enough to explore the road up the mountain, by the time we reached the top we were producing so much water into our improvised bucket collecting system that we decided to return home. This second time all went well and we enjoyed our climb up and over the mountain and arrived in Sakon Nakon in time for lunch. As we approached the centre of the town we were attracted by a large sign on top of a building at a cross roads with an arrow pointing to the 'M and J Hotel'. The 'Mike and Joan Hotel' seemed to be just the place for us and so that is where we ate our lunch. Then we retraced our way back to a ring road where, on the way in, we had noticed a sign for Nakhorn Phanom. Driving along that flat road we were interested to see at various villages along the road quite sizable Roman Catholic Church buildings. The presence of Roman Catholics in this area was probably due to an outreach from the old French Indochina countries of Laos, Cambodia and Vietnam.

Fifteen or so miles before we reached Nakhorn Phanom the road deteriorated into a very uneven dirt track. Road repairs were in process along this stretch of road and as is often the practice in Thailand the whole road surface on both sides of the road had been removed. The road was double track in either direction and it would appear, to the uninitiated, that one double track could have been used as a single track in either direction while the other double track was repaired unhampered by traffic. Then the process could have been reversed in order to repair the other side. However, the preferred method of repair meant that a constant battle was being waged between the traffic, on the one hand, and water tankers spreading water allied with mechanical heavy rollers on the other hand. These water spreaders were trying, to keep the dust from becoming a dust storm, and so preventing traffic moving altogether, and to provide a fleet of steam rollers with a 10 % chance of bedding the road into a flat surface in preparation for the laying of a tar macadam surface. Meanwhile the buses and heavy trucks prevented any such thing from happening and churned out deep ruts and potholes to produce their version of off road driving conditions for 4x4 motorists relishing a challenge or dirt track conditions for motorcycle enthusiasts. Consequently such road repair projects take an extremely long time. We were pleased to make it into the centre of town without bumping stationary or moving objects, turning over, breaking a spring or puncturing a tyre. Nevertheless, we decided that we would try to return by a different route.

The hotel was true to its name (Riverside Hotel) and so was fairly easy to find. Hotel staff were all very friendly and welcoming and we quickly settled in. We enjoyed looking across the river at the dramatic looking and unusual shaped mountains of

Laos which started to rise quite close to the bank on the far side of the river. This was quite strange because on the Thai side there were no mountains in sight and yet the meaning of Nakhorn Phanom is Mountain Capital. After checking in to the hotel we drove back into town and after driving around to get a feel of the layout of the place we drove westwards parallel with the river in an unsuccessful attempt to locate Ho Chi Min's house. Instead we found a large Roman Catholic cathedral with its two spires and large main doors facing in the direction of the river and Laos. When almost out of the town environs we passed, on the left hand side of the road, a very nice building set back in its own grounds on a slight ridge. But that turned out to be a psychiatric hospital and nothing at all to do with Ho Chi Min's abode. Back in town we found a small Baptist church but decided that we would not be able to attend the service there on the following day because we would need a fairly early start home. However, on a later visit we were able to enjoy fellowship with the Christians who worshipped there. They also showed us, on that second visit, where the MSU satellite campus was located.

On the first visit we also drove out of town in an easterly direction still exploring for Ho Chi Min's residence. We came across quite an impressive building, off to the right of the road, but on closer inspection this turned out to be a prison and as soon as we realised this we did not hover around too much! Almost opposite the prison was an Agricultural College and although we drove round its extensive grounds we found no sign of an MSU satellite campus.

It had been interesting exploring Nakhorn Phanom but it was obvious that if we were going to be successful in discovering its past or present prestigious connections then we would need to be armed with much more local know how. Some of the locals from whom we asked directions on this occasion seemed to know that MSU did have some sort of presence in the town but they were not able to give us very detailed advice. No-one we asked could give us the slightest clue as to where Ho Chi Min had lived, so we probably had not met up with any of the resident Vietnamese population, who would almost certainly have had an interest in the history of their former leader. But then again they may have thought we were suspicious looking characters who should be given as little information as possible.

In the morning we started back on our return journey travelling eastwards in roughly the same direction as the river into Mukdahan province and town where we had lunch. A friend of ours, Eva Bennet, had worked there as a missionary in the late 1960s and we knew that there was a small protestant church in Mukdahan, but we could not find it. Continuing our journey in a south easterly direction we drove through part of Amnardjaroen province and on into Yasothorn province. There we changed direction to the north east and so into Roi Et province. This led us on into Mahasarakham province and completed our interesting round trip through previously unexplored territory, but it did not accomplish either of our academic related aims in undertaking the trip.

We repeated this journey on two subsequent occasions. The next occasion we again travelled alone but this time travelled straight through to Nakhorn Phanom on Saturday and attended the Baptist church morning service on Sunday. An American missionary had been responsible under God for founding this church. He was no longer there and the church now had a Thai pastor. The experience of the missionary was a lesson in perseverance. He had worked seemingly unsuccessfully in several parts of Thailand and this was the last place in Thailand that he was going to try and found a church before returning home. This time a church was established and was going from strength to strength without his continued presence which indicates that it was the Lord who was building His Church – and that is how it should be.

Two nurses who attended the service took us, after we had eaten lunch together with the church members, to a school nearby where MSU rented some of the buildings as a temporary base for their operations. So we had found the MSU connection. However, Ho Chi Min's house still remained a mystery. On the way home we stayed overnight in Mukdahan, not such a good hotel as the Riverside in Nakhorn Phanom, and had a good discussion with the pharmacists who owned a nice new pharmacy opposite the hotel. Both husband and wife were pharmacists and had trained at KKU, so we shared some common knowledge and experience. Then we explored the town a little more and ate at a restaurant on the riverside which the pharmacists recommended to us.

The third time we made this journey was early in 2002. This time we travelled with a group of about 40 pharmacy students and two other lecturers, Sunantha and Woottipong. It was a journey to explore some of the culture of the area, stopping at various sites and temples that had been important from the early days of Buddhism in that region, visiting the site of Ho Chi Min's house and the site of the proposed new MSU satellite campus. The Nakhon Phanom Psychiatric Hospital which we had admired on our first visit had a lot of spare undeveloped land adjacent to it and it was proposed that this would be the place where the MSU buildings would be located. It seemed a very good location and had views across to the mountains of Laos.

Ho Chi Min's house was much harder to find. It had been a humble farmer's small single storey wooden dwelling outside the town and close to the river bank. The original house no longer existed but a new house had been built in similar style on the same spot and there was a plaque there explaining that this was the piece of land that Ho Chi Min had farmed and lived on. Just behind the single storey house was a much larger two storey wooden Thai house where the owner of the land lived. His father had lived there before him, at the time Ho Chi Min was living there, and knew him well. The owner of the land still kept in his house various memorabilia relating to Ho Chi Min and he was very happy to explain it to anyone who was interested. We marked our visit by giving him a gift which would remind him of the visit of MSU pharmacy students.

So the mystery of Ho Chi Min's house had been solved at last and I was very pleased about that even though it was not as I had expected. For some reason I had thought that he had been living there under the auspices of the Thai government in a fairly substantial type of property. The impression I had gained was that his house was built in the French colonial style and formed the headquarters of his government in exile. I had even thought that Ho Chi Min's house might form the core building around which the MSU satellite campus would be built. This visit had cleared up both misconceptions.

During our time at MSU we travelled fairly often on the domestic air routes, particularly between Khon Kaen and Bangkok and occasionally to Chiang Mai. While waiting for planes in domestic terminals it is now a very common, but rather disturbing sight, to see rather odd couples consisting of an elderly white man in the tow of a much younger unsophisticated Thai woman. Neither can speak the other's language with any competence, so baby talk and sign language is the sum total of their communication skills. The Thai lady cannot be blamed for her smattering of English, because in fact she is not a well educated person, but probably the daughter of a poor Thai farmer who spent his life hardly making ends meet. Nevertheless, she is the one who is in control and her partner is almost in the position of a toddler with an adult. The difference being that in this case the toddler buys the sweeties. To be fair he too may not be the best educated person to have ever left his country to seek adventure in lands afar. He is utterly out of his depth and often looks somewhat pathetic. How and why do these people get themselves into this ridiculous situation seems to be a good question to ask oneself? We seem to have two people who started off with completely different aspirations and neither would seem to have considered very deeply what it was that made the other seek such a relationship. Let us consider the situation from the man's point of view and the woman's point of view will perhaps become obvious.

His life has probably been spent working at a fairly ordinary type of job with average or less than average pay and he has now reached retirement age. His wife may have died, he has walked out on her, or he was never married and may have only a minimal understanding of the opposite sex. He reviews his situation and thinks his present situation does not look like improving a great deal and decides that what he needs is someone who thinks he is wonderful and will count it a privilege to attend to his every need at little or no cost to himself. Where could he possibly find such Utopia? Then he hears of an organisation that specialises in arranging perfect marriages with wonderful Thai ladies, who are submissive to the nth degree, will think that he's wonderful whatever he does and will take care of his every need. Not being too discerning he swallows the hype, hook line and sinker, and almost before he knows what he is doing he finds himself in Thailand

and discovers to his joy that it is all true. In fact he is shown a whole range of photographs, plus a paragraph describing the exceptional personal characteristics of each of many Thai ladies, who are prepared to snap up his not yet voiced offer of some form of liaison. The introductions and the living together are quickly arranged and before he knows it he has been taken in tow and finds out that the most important thing he can do to keep his wife/partner happy is to give her full instructions of how to access his bank account so that she can look after him properly. Similar to the Prodigal Son he finds that when his money is gone his partner has somehow disappeared as well. This kind of thing also seems to be happening with more educated people as well.

The following is a happily married Thai lady's insight into what she calls interracial marriage. It involves more educated couples than those I have described above. In her discussion of the subject she mentions a Thai lady friend who is desperate to get to England, whereas the uneducated women I described would have been very hard put to survive in England – nevertheless I think some do – but in a desperately unhappy state. This is the Thai lady's letter, written from an address in England, to the Bangkok Post and published as part of 'Postbag', on Friday 11 October 2002.

'My husband and I have witnessed several cases of interracial marriage and we have an English friend who is interested in the possibility. I am a Thai, and even I find it difficult to recommend that he marry a Thai lady.

Thai ladies are caring and well able to look after their husbands in all domestic respects, but at what cost? Is bankruptcy a reasonable price to pay?

No doubt some financial aid to the family is only to be expected; what family wouldn't do that? But the cool, calculating siphoning off of all their husband's wealth to finance houses for in-laws, motorbikes for nephews, sewing machines for sisters-in-law – the list goes on – is ridiculous, and I wonder how many men are aware of the trap that is being laid for them.

I realise that this is a gross generalisation, and that, like my husband and I, there must be many happily married couples, but there is a significant number of cases where this happens.

What has moved me to write all this is a recent phone call from a girl I was at school with in Thailand who is seeking advice in her efforts to marry an Englishman. She confessed on the phone that she was desperate to marry and come to England.

You might think this is a desperate bar-girl making a bid to escape a desperate situation. In fact, this girl is a well-educated person with a respectable job. I don't know whether to contact her fiancé and warn him, or whether to think it serves him right for marrying someone without really knowing her at all.

My point in saying all this is that I, as a Thai lady, am ashamed of these women, and the cool, calculating way they choose their husbands and exploit them. I am ashamed of the culture that has created them. What's happened to Buddhism? What's happened to humility and respect? What's happened to Thailand?

I know that there is another side of the argument, and that it is not only the women that are to blame. "It takes two to tango", as they say in England.

It is a case of culture: the culture of England where a Thai wife is an easy option for many lonely bachelors looking for a wife; the culture of Thailand where for many women, Western men are seen as a resource to be exploited; and the culture of Thailand that has created a situation in which women will do anything to get money for their families, and in which money has become so important.'

That letter is full of insight, especially to the Thai situation, and explains the situation extremely well. It sounds a strong warning to those who treat marriage or liaisons so lightly and see it only as a means to personal gain, without any concern for the misery it may cause their spouse. I hope the practice will soon become much less common as more people learn that these marriages do not work out unless the couple have first built up a natural knowledge, understanding and appreciation of each other over a period of time which then leads into marriage.

July-August 2000 we planned a family holiday in Thailand with Peter and his family and Megan and her family. Joan and I travelled from Aberdeen by our usual route via Amsterdam on 26 July and the other two families flew from Manchester via Copenhagen. Our flight arrived in Bangkok about three hours ahead of the others and we waited for them at the airport and travelled into town together on the airport bus. That turned out to be a bad decision on my part. It took about two hours through the traffic to the Narai Hotel in Silom and the bus did not deliver to hotels, as I had assumed, but rather dropped people off in the vicinity of their hotel. This then left the passengers having to struggle across busy streets with too much baggage to carry comfortably. We would have been better advised to take a minivan. It would have only taken about half an hour via the expressway, delivered us directly to the hotel and would have been cheaper than 12 fares on the airport bus.

The hotel swimming pool was an immediate hit with the families. Early Friday morning Peter, TJ, Hugh, Dicken and I set off for a long tailed boat trip along the Chao Phrya river and a network of canals on the Thonburi side of the river. This was an attempt to repeat a boat trip that I made with Peter just before he flew back to England to school in 1966. The floating market did not now exist to the same extent as in former days, but this time we took in an added attraction in the form of a snake and crocodile farm with some exotic birds and monkeys added in for good measure. Then we proceeded to the boatsheds where the dramatically carved and coloured King's long boats, known as Royal Barges, as used in the annual royal river spectacular, were moored. After a stop off at the Temple of Dawn we crossed to the Royal Palace landing jetty, rehydrated ourselves with bottled drinks and unsuccessfully attempted to go round the Royal Palace. The lads were dressed in shorts and on that occasion did not fancy hiring the long trousers at the gate which would have made them respectable tourists.

A highlight for most of us was a visit for an evening meal to Ban Chiang Restaurant which was located in the house we lived in throughout our four years in Bangkok. The food was excellent and we ate in the part of the house that we used as 'hong rab kaeg', or the room to receive guests. The four main rooms of the house were all set out with tables and chairs and were occupied with people enjoying their food. Outside there were more tables in the garden. It was quite a going concern which was advertised as providing genuine Thai food in an authentic Thai style house. The name of the restaurant was taken from the name of a village in NE Thailand where prehistoric remains have been found.

On Saturday we proceeded by air to Chiang Mai to enjoy Thailand's second city and a stay at my favourite Amari Rincome Hotel with its wonderful food, friendly service and full length swimming pool. The night market is a highlight in Chiang Mai with lots of handmade local products available at reasonable prices. Several of the family had sets of fine clothes made at one of the numerous local tailors and we took the popular trip up Doi Sutheb, the rain forest covered mountain. In order to enter the King's Palace Garden's Mick, Megan, Peter, Laurie, TJ and Hugh hired and donned baggy trousers, or skirts, as appropriate and managed to look the part. On another day we visited the Mae Sae Elephant camp and some took rides through the jungle. Sunday afternoon several of us attended the 5.00 pm English service of the Chiang Mai Community Church which was held in the First

Thai Church building. Joan and I met Mary Cooke an old friend from Central Thailand days.

Our sightseeing was greatly facilitated by Dr. Jaratbhan, the Dean of the Faculty of Pharmacy, making her private Volkswagen minibus with driver, Boon, available to us. Jaratbhan also very generously took us all to the stunningly beautiful Regent Resort Hotel restaurant and showed us the Regent Spa.

Phukhet was our next destination for a few days at the seaside. Megan joined Peter's family for an all day boat trip. Mick, Sam, Aaron, Joan and I took the less adventurous option of life around the hotel. Then it was a flight to Bangkok and on to Khon Kaen to the Raja Orchid Sofitel hotel in Khon Kaen to experience a taste of unexpected five star luxury. Nearly all visitors to Khon Kaen are totally amazed to find such a high class hotel in what they have had described to them as the least developed area of the country. From here we were able to visit Mahasarakham and the University for a day. It was good for the family to see where we lived and worked and for us to be able to show them the encouraging developments that were taking place and that many things were probably better than they had expected. The time in NE Thailand was all too short for some. Peter wrote about this part of the holiday 'The real Thailand was here, but just out of reach. Yonder the Mekong river, the Lao and the Khmer.' After three days we were back in Bangkok where we could attend a morning service at Christ Church, Convent Road, and Megan could visit the maternity unit where she was born in the Bangkok Christian Hospital, Silom Road. Then the evening of 13 August we said our farewells and they returned overnight to England. Monday 14 August was the Queen's Birthday Holiday and we spent this in Khon Kaen. On Tuesday we returned to Mahasarakham, after what for us was an enjoyable holiday of many memorable experiences and a time of mutual getting to know each other better. We were grateful to the Lord that a complicated holiday had worked out very well.

The following summer Peter and family, Paul and family, Rose and family and Megan and family coordinated their holidays in the same area of Cornwall. They could choose to meet up with each other or go their separate ways and that on the whole was very successful. Ann and family were attending a church house party and so could not make it. In the summer of 2002 all five families, together with Joan and me, holidayed for a week in the same refurbished farmhouse complex in Brittany. There were 34 of us altogether. Joan and I enjoyed it tremendously; it meant a great deal to us to be able to have a week together with the whole family. We spent different days with different families or groupings of families and most days we all met up together on the same beach in the middle to late afternoon.

CHAPTER 11

CHRISTIAN FELLOWSHIP

Having fellowship with fellow believers in Christ is very important for Christians and we seek to have such fellowship wherever we go. Soon after arriving in Mahasarakham we linked up with a small group of about six Christians, basically from two families, the pastor's family and another family. We met with them on Sundays when we were in Mahasarakham. Pastor Prasarn was from Udorn, a city about 120 miles North West of Mahasarakham, but still in the same NE region. He had studied at the Bangkok Bible College and had then obtained practical experience working with John and Virginia Casto, OMF missionaries at Uthaithani. Thus he had quite an OMF background. Now he was supported by the American Church of the Nazarene. The church met in a rented house about half a mile from the town centre. Pastor Nipon of the Khon Kaen Chinese

Church had recommended this group of Christians to us. In our first two years in Mahasarakham we often needed to visit Khon Kaen at the weekend and would then attend the Chinese Church there. In the 1980s when we first attended services there, Chinese was still used with a translation into Thai, or vice versa. Now the services were always in Thai. Quite a few lecturing staff and students from KKU attended the church. This was not the case with the Mahasarakham church, but as time passed a few more people started coming along. In 1999 the decision was made to rent a double fronted 'shop house' or literally one of a 'terrace of rooms' (hong thaew), along the side of the Roi Et road on the edge of Mahasarakham. This was on the other side of town from the university which was off the road to Kalasin. The double shop area was used as a meeting place and the upstairs was used both as living accommodation and for 'Sunday school'. Twenty or so people would attend the Sunday morning services and also about as many children. Several of those who came for a while and made a useful contribution to the 'church' later moved away in search of work elsewhere as work in the NE after the economic crisis was difficult to find. Others had health problems which made their attendance irregular. Sometimes there would be a student, or two, from the Teachers College, or from MSU. One or two families from surrounding villages started to come along. They had believed in Christ through listening to a half hour local radio service, for which the church had supplied the tapes and paid the fee for the air time for about the previous two years.

The pattern of the Sunday morning would be as follows. First there would be a time of prayer, followed by an interactive Bible study, led by Prasarn. All would join in with these. Then a worship service followed, usually led by one of the Christian ladies, with Prasarn being responsible for the preaching. Occasionally I would preach. This was mostly when Prasarn was away involved with a part of his study for a Masters degree in Theology, or when he was attending some special meeting. The service was followed by a communal meal and general discussion. It was at these times that we were able to discuss some of the things that Prasarn had on his mind and was praying about. In March 2000 when it was approaching the time that we were planning to return to the UK for a break and to arrange practice placements in the Aberdeen area for some of our PharmD students Prasarn made the following request. He said he was praying about having special English classes in the church property during the long vacation March – June and he felt that he should have a native English speaker, perhaps a young person or student. Prasarn said that he would like me to provide him with such a teacher from the UK. For his part he would provide free accommodation at the church. I explained to him that this was very unlikely as students in the UK were not on holiday at that time. Furthermore it would be very unlikely that a young person would have the cash to pay an expensive airfare from UK to Thailand for just two months. I went on further to say that it would be too much to expect a young person to have the confidence to teach English on their own and at the same time adapt to a new country, culture, climate, food and language. Nevertheless I promised that we would pray about it and see what arose when I returned to Aberdeen. I will now quote from our Strategic Prayer Letter No. 55 May 2000.

'On arriving home, Dr. Paul Wraight, who lives less than a mile from us in Aberdeen contacted us to say that his son Tim, who was having a year out after finishing school, to teach English at a school in Kampheng Phet in NW Thailand, was looking for something useful to do during his long vacation. To cut a long story short Tim ended up in far away Mahasarakham teaching English daily to four different age groups of children/young people. Pastor Prasarn now has friendly contact with large numbers of children living around the church. His own English has improved considerably. Four of the children were at Sunday school and church last Sunday (14 May) and four older ones had attended a Bible study earlier. We believe your many prayers about the church situation were involved in bringing these events into being. This also gives us an example of experiencing God answering specific prayer in a way beyond our imaginations. We were privileged to see the pieces all gradually fitting into place as Paul kept us informed of Tim's movements in Thailand when he received emails from Tim. Joan and I (and Paul and Meg, Tim's parents) had front row seats watching what God was doing through Tim and

Pastor Prasarn. This should encourage us to know that God is also working in all the other situations that you are praying about even though we cannot see the answers unfold step by step. In fact some answers may be instantaneous and others take time before we are aware of the answers.'

Building a church building was also a subject we discussed fairly often. In the summer Prasarn was able to buy a plot of land down a side road just off the main Roi Et road and about a quarter of a mile on the way back into town from the 'shop houses'. In the autumn of 2000 we had an idea of the possible design of a suitable two storey building and the projected costs. The plan was to build the church in the first half of 2001. Through my responsibilities at the university I had gained some experience of the design and price of small buildings in Mahasarakham and was convinced that Prasarn and his proposed builder had underestimated the costs by about 200,000 Baht. Joan and I started praying that the Lord would supply this. I happened to be at a Deacons Court and Kirk Session meeting at my church Gilcomston South in the late autumn. The subject of a special Christmas offering was discussed but there was no obvious need that was made known. I decided that I would not mention the need at Mahasarakham unless I was specifically asked. Then Mike Strudwick, the session clerk, asked me if I could suggest any special need. The result was that the Mahasarakham Church Building was the main subject of the Christmas appeal and that about 202,000 Baht was subsequently given to Prasarn and his building committee. Slightly more than that amount had been given by the folk at Gilcomston and the surplus was given to another need, not in Thailand, that had also been identified. The Lord had again provided through his people, and in addition to supporting the work of the church in Mahasarakham through prayer, the Christians of Gilcomston had now been able to give material support. Thus there is an additional bond between the two churches. Joan and I were privileged to be present at the first service in the new two storey church building in Mahasarakham on 17 June 2001. We wrote an account of the church building in our Strategic Prayer Letter No. 60 of July 2001 and I quote from that letter a short description of the church.

'The walls of the building are painted outside and inside in pale green and the floors throughout are tiled with pale green tiles. All the painting, including doors and windows, and the tiling was paid for by a special Christmas offering from Gilcomston South Church in Aberdeen. The steps up the front of the church and the roof tiling are deep blue. There is a red handrail at the sides of the first flight of steps and a red cross on a special turret over the front of the church. This was a gift from the building contractor who is a Christian. The cross is covered with fluorescent material which is lit up by two spotlights during darkness. The whole effect is very pleasing and it is one of very few such church buildings in the whole of NE Thailand. Costs so far are £8000 for land and £17000 for building. The top floor is for Sunday services and special meetings and the ground floor has the Pastor's office, two small suites of living accommodation, a kitchen, a library and an open fronted shade room for use as a communal dining area after the services and to be used for nursery accommodation throughout the week.......It is also planned to have the church building the centre for an externally funded Christian 'Compassion Project' to support local poor children through their schooling, which many families cannot afford and to link them with the church at least on Sundays. Wisdom is needed that the church buildings are used in the best way to further the Lord's work in Mahasarakham in His way. The buildings are themselves a testimony to the fact that the Lord is at work and represent a resource for carrying out God's work.' The church was officially opened at the end of August.

The other area of Christian fellowship we wanted to share was with any Christian students or staff at the university. Theoretically in a population of several thousand there should be 10-20 Christians but we had not been able to meet up with any. We had mentioned in our Prayer Letter of August 1999 that; 'It would be good to find a Christian or two...' Nothing happened for a while but on Wednesday February 16 the following year we were surprised by the visit of two Thai Christian Students (TCS) staff workers, Nic and Jim (two ladies; these are their nicknames, which have no connection with western names, but just transliterate like that!). They had been helping with special children's meetings at a small church in the district town of Chiang Yeun about 30 miles away. The church was a daughter church of the original Thai church in Khon Kaen. Accompanying Nic and Jim were Ta! and Bai. Ta! was a recent graduate in computing of Khon Kaen University and had been a member of the TCS student group there. He was now the Pastor of the Chiang Yeun church and Bai was his assistant. They had a first year Humanities girl student with them, who belonged to a small church at the district town of Kosumpisai, about 20 miles away. We prayed together in my office and arranged to meet with the two fellows and the girl student on the following Wednesday at 12 noon in the central student canteen. They thought that there were two or three first year students in the Faculty of Science who were Christians and they would invite them to come along. In the event just the three of them came but it was very encouraging having our first meeting together. We prayed and shared how the Lord was working in our lives and situations. The next meeting was arranged for 1 March. Just Ta! and Pum (the girl student) were present, together with Joan and I, but again we had an encouraging time of Bible study, prayer and sharing. The next week nine of us were present. These included three first year students; Juk, engineering, Muay, biological sciences, and Pum, humanities. The others were Ta! with three of his church helpers, Bai, Daeng and Pim. It was again an encouraging time and afterwards they gave out tracts to students in and around the canteen. This was the last meeting of the academic year and we agreed to meet again in June. Pum hoped to attend a

Youth With A Mission (YWAM) discipleship training course at Khon Kaen for quite a large proportion
of her vacation. By the way, all the names quoted
above are nicknames.

A small but important start had been made but it
was not proving to be at all easy. We could not put a
great deal of input into contacting and getting to
know students. I had meetings on just about every
day of the week. A lot of preparation and discussion
was involved with faculty policy and the day to day
administration of the faculty, with many documents
written in Thai to digest and on many occasions to
authorise with my signature, was very demanding.

We met up with the Christian students again at
the beginning of the academic year on 23 June and
they arranged to have weekly meetings. The following week we started our travels to return to Aberdeen
for the PharmD Practice Placements in community
pharmacy. It was 24 August before we were able to
attend the MSU Christian student meeting again. By
that time it was obvious the students were meeting
under the auspices of YWAM. Several of the students
sported YWAM tee shirts and they had a large banner
with YWAM Mahasarakham University Student
Group printed on it. A Korean lady YWAM worker
based in Khon Kaen, Tian, was leading the group. A
few months later Tian moved over to Mahasarakham
and rented two small properties in the centre of town,
one to be used as a hostel for male students and one
for female students. Tian also linked up with the
Mahasarakham Church of the Nazarene. Since we
ourselves were not able to give the time that was

needed to nurture the Christian students the YWAM involvement was helpful and we joined in with the YWAM meetings as best we were able when we were free. Various YWAM teams visited from Korea, America and a mixed team from several different Western and Asian countries. These teams would also have an international input into our church services when they visited.

The following year Campus Crusade for Christ teams started visiting Mahasarakham for meetings with students and in the villages surrounding Mahasarakham. These teams consisted mostly of Christian students from other parts of Thailand and they stayed in the church accommodation while in Mahasarakham. Thus the church and the student witness were being mutually supportive. In addition the church building has proved to be very useful for occasional joint meetings of the leaders from the other two small congregations in Mahasarakham town together with another on the way to Roi Et. It has been used on at least one occasion for a series of joint meetings for the four congregations. Later it was also used as the centre for a 'Compassion Project' to help eighty local schoolchildren from poor families.

In April 2002 a young Thai couple, working with Campus Crusade, came to Mahasarakham with the desire to reach out to students and Pastor Prasarn welcomed them and helped them to find suitable accommodation to rent.

Thus the church is having a very positive supportive role for many Christian activities in addition to the Sunday morning services. It was a great privilege for us to be associated with the development of this work.

CHAPTER 12

CONSOLIDATION OF THE FACULTY

It was a great encouragement to have the two year BSc Public Health Curriculum, the two year PharmD Curriculum, the six year PharmD curriculum, the Faculty of Pharmacy and Health Sciences, the Unipharm Project and the Unipure project all formerly accepted and proceeding in our first 20 months at MSU. Consolidation of the Faculty was now needed. An important but almost hidden part of the consolidation process was strengthening the English conversation and comprehension skills of the academic and administrative staff. This was essential if staff were going to proceed to PhD study, attend and participate in International Conferences, benefit from visits of English speaking academics and contribute to international teaching programmes such as the President's dream of an International

Masters Degree in Public Health.

Joan was a great help in this area providing conversation and comprehension classes with a native English speaker and put in a lot of effort to develop her own skills in helping the staff in these areas. In August 1999 we produced a book 'Polish Your English Skills' plus accompanying audio tapes to be used by our staff and our PharmD students. Some individuals made quite a marked improvement, the majority would not put in the effort needed outside of class and so did not improve as much as we would have hoped. Usually those who progressed best were those who had some short term or mid term goal such as an examination in English in which they needed to achieve a certain grade. The PharmD students were motivated because they hoped to spend five weeks or so in the UK on a Pharmacy Practice work placement and would need good English in order to benefit from that. We were able to have five days at the beginning of November when they had a minimum of one hour of English each day. We would often use passages from the Bible which gave a good opportunity to test comprehension and form the basis for discussion. Since Christmas was approaching we studied parts of the Christmas story and on several occasions listened to and even sang along with carols from a CD.

At the close of our final teaching period in November I read the following passage to them and then asked each one a question to test their listening comprehension.

Some Reasons Why Christmas is a Joyful Season and Important for Everyone

Christmas is a joyful season because it is the time we remember God's great gift of His Son Jesus Christ who left heaven and was born into this world 2000 years ago to be our Saviour. Because God gave us His wonderful gift we also give gifts to each other at Christmas time. We are happy to give and receive gifts. You might ask 'What can we do to show our appreciation of God's wonderful gift to us?' The only gift we can give God is ourselves. Also we can give joy to God by accepting His gift of Jesus as our Saviour from sin and giving Him control of our lives. This gift of Jesus was His great expression of His love to all men and women.

God sent His Son into the world because He loved all people and wanted them to know Him personally. Jesus taught that only through knowing Him can we know God as our Heavenly Father. This is something we can understand with our minds. It is also something we can experience in our hearts and lives.

Questions:
Can you tell me two reasons why Christmas is a joyful time?
What does the passage say is the only gift we can give God? Why do you think that is?
How can we give joy to God?
What does God's gift of His Son teach us about God?

Does God only love good people?
What did Jesus teach was the way through which we could know God as our Heavenly Father?

The passage tells us that 'This is something we can understand with our minds. It is also something we can experience in our hearts and lives.' What is the difference?
(Theory and practice).

During this time in Mahasarakham I also produced a small book 'English for Research' which was to form the basis of a course of the same name to be taught as part of the PharmD programme in the following October (2000).

The seven PharmD students were back at the university in January 2000 for the introductory courses to two more modules of their course and we again spent time teaching them English. Staff numbers had been continuously augmented by one means and another and now stood at 35 staff working in the faculty and ten or so studying for higher degrees. About 12 of these staff were lecturers in public health, six were working in administration and the rest were pharmacy lecturers. The most useful way of obtaining additional pharmacy staff was to apply through the University for Government Scholarships which were provided to help develop new subject areas. In a good year we might be successful in obtaining four such scholarships. These were then advertised externally, in the subject areas that we would need to teach in two or three year's time, but in which we did not yet have any lecturers appointed. The successful applicant would be offered the two year scholarship to study for a master degree on the basis that they returned to the faculty as a lecturer on completion of their studies. In this way we were able to attract a high calibre of ambitious young staff and to have them come to us as lecturers already in possession of a Masters degree.

As a faculty we looked forward to the new entry in June 2000 which should provide us with about 40 full time pharmacy students on the six year PharmD, a total of 15-20 two year part time PharmD students and a total of about 350 two year part time BSc Public Health students.

The major problem we faced was the lack of dedicated accommodation for the faculty. On 25 February it was announced that we would not be getting any government money for a faculty building in the next financial year beginning October 2000. That meant that October 2001 was now the next opportunity for obtaining building funds from the Government and that was 20 months away. When the funds were made available it would probably take two years to complete a faculty building, so the very earliest we could expect a faculty building was now four years away. This was the third year our hopes had been lifted and dashed. They were lifted because every year we were told that we were being given top priority by the University. I know that we were in the Administrative Committee's documentation at the top of the buildings request list that was submitted to the Government for funding. For one reason or another we missed out on the relatively small amount of funding that was granted.

The situation was not yet critical as the majority of the first year of the six year PharmD course would be taught in the Faculty of Science. One large new faculty building for the physical sciences had been completed and another large building for the biological sciences was under construction. The public health students also had part of their course taught in the Faculty of Science laboratories. Personally I found the lack of any prospect of funding for a faculty building in the foreseeable future quite discouraging and potentially very serious. It meant that I was repeatedly trying to negotiate for promises of temporary space in existing new faculty buildings; such space was often surplus to the current requirements of the faculty concerned. Several such agreements between the University President, Vice Presidents and Deans concerned fell through almost as soon as they had been made. The frustrating thing was that people would agree in the meeting to a particular course of action and then return privately to see the President and persuade him that some other course of action would be better. This would result in the original joint decision, by all parties concerned, being overturned. It then seemed to be accepted that it was my responsibility to renegotiate a new arrangement, starting from scratch, and with no guaranteed support from anyone. I sometimes referred to this as going round in circles and often said, within the faculty at least, that I did not like 'going round in circles' and in fact, I was not going to spend my time going round in circles. Pressure to go round in circles happened all the time. We would have a meeting of the Faculty Administrative Committee and make decisions concerning the running of the Faculty. Within a few days someone would come to see me and tell me that they had a better idea about something that had been decided at the recent meeting. This change of opinion was often because, on further consideration, the person concerned did not like the implications of the decision taken for their own workload or responsibilities. They then worked out a way of how to reorganise things so that someone else would become responsible for these things. I would refuse to change, explaining that a joint decision had been made and we must now put it into operation, at least for several months, before I would consider a rearrangement. The other possible way that lecturers might try to get things changed was to bring up the business that had been decided on at the previous meeting for reconsideration at the beginning of the subsequent meeting, even though that business was not an agenda item. I realise that I was really fighting a cultural characteristic here and could not expect to change the lifetime habits of those I worked with. Nevertheless, I did try to operate a different system within the faculty. Almost anything that I can think of that is done in Thailand, as the result of a decision making process, goes through a process of subsequent modification and change. The Thai are naturally extremely flexible in their lifestyle and way of doing things, except where it involves government bureaucracy. This can be an asset, for example when travelling in Thailand flexibility of mind and action is rather essential and without it one would get very stressed. In other situations flexibility may result in some quite dangerous situations. For example it is a common occurrence for concrete poles carrying high voltage electricity to be inappropriately sited particularly in relation to the traffic flow on newly constructed roads. This has led to many vehicles having collisions with the poles and plunging the surrounding area into a state of chaos due to a sudden loss of electric power. The reason for the poles being placed such as to interfere with traffic flow may be hard to fathom but it is often related to the road having been originally constructed with a different line or width from how it subsequently was made. If the poles for the electric cables had been put in to conform with the original road they would subsequently be out of place after road modifications were made. It may then take months before the appropriate expertise and equipment are assembled to realign the poles. Meanwhile the chance of vehicles colliding with poles is quite high, especially at night time when many vehicles do not have lights in fully functioning order. I read in a newspaper that insurance companies and the electricity companies were getting together to try and devise ways to reduce the number of crashes into badly sited electricity poles. Such accidents were proving very expensive to both parties and this expense was seen to be something which should be preventable with foresight and planning and all parties concerned sticking to the original construction plans. It is too early to say whether this proposed collaboration makes an impact on reducing this type of practice and in reducing accidents.

On the positive side of faculty development; the University Community Pharmacy – Unipharm – at the edge of the night market, opened for business in the middle of March. This was well on schedule and a real morale booster, not only for us as a faculty, but also for the whole university. On the other hand the University Drinking Water Project – Unipure was proceeding quite slowly and we were going round in many circles. A concerted effort was needed to ensure that it did not get completely bogged down in bureaucracy and university politics.

In March 2000 I was preparing to attend the next two yearly meeting of the Thai-American Consortium of Thai Pharmacy Faculties and American Colleges of Pharmacy. It was planned that this would take place in Miami, Florida at the beginning of April and I planned to travel to the UK, leave Joan there, go on to Florida for the Conference and then return to UK to collect Joan so that we could travel back together to Thailand. This worked out well and we returned to Thailand at the beginning of May in order to make preparations for the beginning of the next academic year. We also had to prepare for four of the first seven PharmD students to travel to Aberdeen, for a week's introductory course at RGU, and four weeks Pharmacy Practice work placement in local community pharmacies. There should have been five students, but about two weeks before they were due to leave, Teerawut came to see me to tell me he had just been diagnosed as having oesophageal cancer. Teerawut was in his early thirties and had been experiencing great difficulties in swallowing food for some time. Two male relatives had previously died of oesophageal cancer at about the same age that he was then. We decided that he would have to withdraw from the Aberdeen visit and I had a very good opportunity to talk to him about spiritual things and he assured me that he was trusting in Christ for salvation and to take care of him. I prayed with him and then he left.

When I was away in Florida our university president had visited Australia. He had taken with him three lecturers from the Faculty of Pharmacy and Health Sciences who had major teaching responsibilities on our public health course. These lecturers were Miss Sunantha, Dr. Yanyong and Mr. Songkramchai. They went to visit Wollongong University, New South Wales, to discuss the possibility of setting up a joint International Master Degree in Public Health. This was to be taught at MSU, but with a major input from Wollongong, particularly in curriculum design and providing lecturers to help teach the course. There was also the hope that Wollongong would offer one or more scholarships for our staff to undertake a PhD in public health at Wollongong University. Yanyong would likely be the MSU staff member who would act as Course Director and Songkramchai would hopefully be the first beneficiary of any scholarship. Sunantha had been involved with the MSU Public Health degree from its initiation and so she was also a necessary member of the party. It was however a complete surprise to me to find out about this visit when I returned to MSU. I was also told that a Professor in Public Health from Wollongong would visit, 14-15 June, to discuss with me how we could cooperate to set up an International Master Degree programme in Health Administration to commence in 2001 and a Master in Public Health to commence in June 2002. It was suggested that an added attraction of the cooperation would be that the graduates would receive a Master Degree from each university. The thought was that we would attract students from Thailand, Laos, Cambodia and Vietnam.

International Programmes were seen to be highly desirable programmes for Thai universities to organise and they increased the reputation of the university to the general public. The International programme did not necessarily require cooperation with an overseas university, but such cooperation was seen as an added benefit because it added to the reputation of the programme, especially if two degrees were on offer. Mounting such a programme also indicated that the lecturers who taught the course were fluent in spoken English and had established a wide reputation for their expertise in their subject areas. These latter two points gave me considerable concern because neither could be said of the majority of our lecturers in public health. This would mean that, at least in the early years, we would have to rely heavily on lecturers from Wollongong.

The visit by Professor Dennis Calvert from Wollongong went very well and we seemed to have reached an agreement which covered the points above. It was later, when he returned home to Wollongong and discussed things further with his staff that it became obvious that we at MSU were being required to provide a greater input than originally agreed. This resulted in the agreement being shelved for the time being with the possibility of reactivation when MSU staff had developed further expertise. All this took a considerable amount of time but did not result in any tangible benefits. I had seen this type of thing happen before, with the discussions with the Dean from the University of Florida. Unfortunately it is not often possible to meet the aspirations of both universities and at the same time provide an outstanding product that will greatly benefit and be attractive to prospective students.

The pressure was now on the PharmD students planning to travel to Aberdeen to obtain all their necessary documentation in order in time to travel. I was pleased that they organised this themselves as being ready in time was a close call for one or two of them. Nevertheless, Manote, Wilawan, Thanyarat and Phayom, plus the wife of Manote, Saisini (a dentist), all arrived in Aberdeen on 7 July as planned. We had travelled to Aberdeen a few days ahead of them so that we would be there to welcome them and take care of their arrangements. In addition to their study week at RGU and their practice placements, arranged by Mrs Sandra Hutchinson, we had the opportunity to show them some of the beautiful countryside along the River Dee. They also came to Gilcomston South Church of Scotland with us where they met our minister Dominic Smart and were able to get to know some of our friends such as Tom Scott, Irene Smith and Pat Dickson, who were pleased to invite them home to meals. Suchida and Naeti, Thai PhD students at RGU, were also a great help. The visit worked out very well academically and they enjoyed themselves as well. We returned to Thailand about 10 days ahead of them to join some of our family for a holiday as described in the section 'Travelling in Isarn'. When the family visited MSU we met up with the PharmD students again and Peter gave them a lecture on the treatment of asthma and the pharmacist's involvement with the patient in the management of asthma. My next teaching commitment to this group combined with the second intake of two year PharmD students was the course 'English for Research.'

We thought there was a need for a 'Pharmacy Assistants' course to be developed by an appropriate academic institution because a 'Pharmacy Technicians' course which had previously been offered in Bangkok had been discontinued. The 'Assistants' course was intended principally for the community pharmacy situation whereas the 'Technicians' course had been primarily for the hospital situation. We hoped to obtain information about similar courses in the UK. I also needed to start negotiations with another UK School of Pharmacy to provide a similar course to that which had been provided for our four PharmD students at RGU in July. It was not considered possible for RGU School of Pharmacy to provide further courses for our students, which was quite a disappointment, especially as I had been used to providing courses for many overseas pharmacists during my time at RGU and RGU had the reputation of collaborating with Thai universities. Difficulties were also arising with communicating satisfactorily with the responsible staff at RGU concerning Nusaraporn's and Sunantha's PhD progress. Discussions were urgently needed with several senior people to try and get these things cleared up and to ensure that neither Nusaraporn nor Sunantha were disadvantaged. (In fact these discussions took place during our next visit to Aberdeen and after a few administrational adjustments those of us then involved were able to work well together and subsequently Nusaraporn and Sunantha were both successful in obtaining their PhDs keeping to their original timescales. With the completion of these two PhDs I had been directly associated with 13 lecturers from Thailand who had successfully completed RGU PhDs. Eight of these were from the University of Khon Kaen).

On Monday 9 October we left MSU and travelled to Bangkok where we stayed with Woranoot, at the Bangkok Christian College. When visiting Woranoot we would catch up with news about Tippawan, her sister, who was now working in China. Tippawan was initially interested in helping children with disabilities and worked at an orphanage run by Christians. Subsequently Tippawan taught English and Thai at a Chinese University for a year before founding and heading up an influential and successful educational programme to combat the spread of HIV/Aids.

Suwatt and Yenjai took us out for an evening meal on Tuesday and Suwatt drove us to the airport on Wednesday evening. The next day Iain collected us at Dyce airport, Aberdeen. Tom had put the heating on in our house so all was nice and warm and in order for us when we arrived. Our friends had looked after us well and provided almost seamless care from door to door once again. The next day, 13 October, was the 45th anniversary of my starting National Service. I always remember that with gratitude to the Lord for all his blessings during those eventful two years. It was very good missionary training and we saw the Lord working in many ways. Also on arriving home we sent out our Strategic Prayer Letter No.57 to keep our praying friends abreast of developments. The letter had been written in Thailand just before travelling home.

While at home we were again able to get our business attended to and visit several of the family. Preliminary arrangements were made with Dr. Geoff Hall to have our next five day PharmD introductory course on community pharmacy in the UK taught at De Montfort University, Leicester. Travelling on 13 November from Ann and family in Leicester to Megan in Lytham St. Anne's we diverted to Wingerworth, near Chesterfield, to visit the daughter of an elderly lady (Mae Ba!) we knew at the Mahasarakham church. Mrs. Thairat had married an Englishman. Unfortunately she was out at work but I met her husband who was very friendly. Previously I had been unable to contact Thairat by phone, but after that visit she phoned me in Aberdeen and so I was able to take back news to her mother.

We flew back to Thailand overnight on Tuesday 5 December and rested up at Woranoot's flat, at the Bangkok Christian College, before travelling on to MSU on Friday 8 December. I wanted to be back for the preliminaries and the actual graduation of the first intake of public health students on 11 December. These were the first students to graduate from our faculty and it represented a milestone in the Faculty's development. Another milestone was achieved at the same time when the Unipure project was functioning in time to supply the University's own drinking water for sale on the day of the Graduation Ceremony. More development was needed to increase the production and marketing capacity but a start had been made and maximum publicity obtained for the product.

On Wednesday 20 December we received an email from Tom Scott, who kindly kept an eye on our house, that there had been a break in to our home at 6.30 pm on Tuesday by three men. They had smashed two of the wire reinforced glass panes in our outer back door so that they could loosen the top and bottom bolts and push the double door open, even though it was still locked. This must have produced thousands of minute pieces of glass on the porch floor. They were then faced with another door with a large glass pane at the top. This time they ignored the glass and smashed in the wooden panel at the bottom of the door, which they would then have to crawl under, thus getting many pieces of glass into their clothes. These were then shed in every room of the house and proved very hard to remove from the carpets with a vacuum cleaner. They also smashed open the locked garden gate to leave themselves an escape route. All this made a tremendous amount of noise and our next door neighbour at that time heard them and took a peep over the wall to see what was happening. She realised that a burglary was in process and, together with her husband, phoned the police and directed them to the house. One lot of police came up the back lane to the garden gate and another one drove his patrol car up the terrace to the front door. This policeman got a glimpse of one of the burglars through the front bedroom window and realised that he was one of Grampian Police's most wanted criminals, so he radioed for reinforcements. The police seem to have allowed the burglars leave the house with their spoils and arrested them as they were loading them into a car. Tom was eventually tracked down, attending a concert at the Music Hall, and he kindly stayed in our house that night and arranged for repairs to be done in order to make the house secure. We had to see to the finer details when we returned home. Meanwhile we had to communicate with the police telling them from which place in the house each of the stolen items was taken and the value of each item. They then included all this information in a statement which was sent to us to sign and return. The stolen items, which the police called 'Productions', were kept in the police station but were under the control of the Procurator Fiscal.

When the three burglars were charged with their crime they pleaded 'Not guilty!' and so that meant they had to await a trial date sometime in June 2001 and our 'Productions' had to be kept until then. Predictably the plea was changed to 'Guilty!' just before the trial was due. We have no idea what their sentence was and could not find out from the police or the Procurator Fiscal's department. Neither could we get our property released, although at one stage I was allowed to check the personal mail stolen from the doormat to see if it contained anything that needed dealing with urgently! It was not until August that we were able to retrieve our property and that was after many telephone calls had been made to the Procurator Fiscal's department. On Wednesday 1 August I phoned the Procurator Fiscal's office in the morning enquiring about our property and, as I was still not getting a satisfactory answer, I said, that 'If our 'Productions' were not released by Friday then I would proceed to make a formal complaint'. That afternoon I received a phone call to tell me that I could collect the 'Productions' from the Central Police Station on Thursday morning!

It can be seen that the Lord overruled at the time of the break in. The police said that it was very rare that they ever caught burglars red handed and that this case was really quite unique. They would never have expected to catch the seasoned criminal leading the burglary in this way and they were absolutely delighted. All our property was eventually returned to us unharmed. Tom was available to efficiently deal with making the house secure. The burglars were brought to justice. We were very thankful to the Lord.

I believe the Lord does watch over His children and servants. People cannot attack us or our property with impunity. They will be brought to justice in God's way and in His time.

Meantime at MSU I was involved in; teaching; spending quite a few days helping Khon Kaen University lecturers write up their research into research papers for publication in international journals (quite successful!); heading up a faculty representation at part of the funeral rites for the father of one of our lecturers – Sunantha taking my place for the specifically Buddhist part; producing 'Course Descriptors' in English for the 'Pharmacy Assistants Course'; translating 'Course Descriptors' for the 'Thai Traditional Medicine Degree' from Thai to English; attending special Christmas Services at the Church in Mahasarakham and the Church in Khon Kaen; organising a faculty Christmas party at which we sang many carols accompanied by a computer Karioke programme; taking part in an evangelistic student Christmas party together with about 10 Korean students and Tian (YWAM), and Ta! with about 20 young people from his church in Chiang Yeun; attending the University New Year's party on 27 December and having good conversations with two young lecturers; helping Sunantha and Nusaraporn with PhD documentation for RGU; signing several hundred Faculty New Year Cards; sending and receiving numerous emails and Christmas cards. All in all an opportunity to get many disparate jobs done while taking part in special Christmas and New Year celebrations and generally being an integral part of the University life and the life of Christians in Mahasarakham and Khon Kaen. Demanding but fulfilling and a real privilege for us to be generally so accepted and welcomed in all the variety of activities taking place. We were now at home and functioning quite well in Isarn!

On Friday 29 December we drove to Nakhorn Phanom, on the Mekong River, and stayed at the Riverside Hotel. It was on this visit we were able to attend the Baptist Church 10.00 am and 11.00 am Sunday services followed by lunch and fellowship. We travelled back home via Mukdahan, Yasothorn and Roi Et on the following Tuesday.

A week later I had a discussion with Dr. Pavich about his ideas as to whether he would want me to take a further contract after my current one was completed on 30 September. I was particularly concerned that I would need to be in Aberdeen for a considerable part of the next contractual year to work on the third edition of the textbook 'Pharmaceutical Practice', which I co-edited with Dr. Arthur Winfield. The publishers (Churchill Livingstone) were very pleased with the uptake of the second edition in many countries and it had also been translated into Chinese and was being translated into Thai. We had already started discussions about a third edition. The publishers had surveyed the opinions of many lecturing staff and students in the UK and other countries and the detailed comments they had received were overwhelmingly favourable. Dr. Pavich said that he wanted me to stay at MSU for another year and that I could work out my visits so as to suit my schedule of work. An advantage to MSU would be that I would write and edit the book while holding the position of Dean at the university and this designation would be acknowledged in the title pages of the book. MSU did not have the possibility of many of its staff writing textbooks which had an international circulation. So we made that decision, to stay on, in principle but decided to wait until later to see how it would best work out in practice. I was not too comfortable about being away from MSU for a long period while still holding the position as Dean. On 2 August Arthur Winfield, who was visiting back from Kuwait University, and I had a meeting in Aberdeen with Mrs.Ellen Green and Ms. Sian Jarman, representing the publishers. Arthur and I agreed to co-edit the third edition of the book and our proposed overall format for the book, the chapter titles and length of chapters, which we had previously agreed together, were now accepted by the publishers. It was then the responsibility of Arthur and I to make arrangements with prospective authors to write specific chapters with a view to receiving their chapters by 1 May 2002 and submitting the edited chapters as a complete book to the publishers by 30 September. Proofs would be corrected around about the following spring and the projected publication date would be September 2003. Arthur and I started work along the lines indicated straight away and I also started work on revising my chapters and writing a new one.

The book length would be about 550 printed pages consisting of 43 illustrated chapters and six appendices, so it was quite an undertaking.

In January 2001 work was begun on the church building in Mahasarakham and a group of a dozen or so mostly fairly elderly Americans, from a Nazarene church or possibly several Nazarene churches, arrived on 17 January to give a boost to the work. They stayed in the best hotel that Mahasarakham had to offer at that time, the New Pattana Hotel in the centre of town, and had their lunch at the rented 'shop house' church building which was about a quarter of a mile from the new building site. Their building contribution was mostly by way of encouragement to the local Christians and builders, but it was interesting, even surprising, for the local people to see elderly Americans involved in manual work in the heat of Thailand. Fortunately January is mostly the least hot month in Mahasarakham. A recently arrived Nazarene Missionary, who was in the middle of his language study in Bangkok, accompanied them to Mahasarakham. I was involved as interpreter on several semi-formal occasions.

In the Faculty we were now involved in producing the curriculum for Masters Degree programmes in Public Health. This was quite a complicated process because we wanted to have five different tracks leading to five different Masters Degrees and the option that each track could be studied in Thai or in English. The object in this was that it would make it easier to eventually cooperate with an overseas university to mount a joint International Masters

Degree programme. We were also involved in producing the weighty documentation required for a
Quality Assurance (QA) Internal Audit of the
Faculty. This exercise followed the procedures developed for University Teaching Quality Assurance
Assessment in Scotland. By some quirk of circum-
stance I found that UK bureaucracy had caught up
with me in Thailand. As a faculty we adopted the
policy of Total Quality Management with Continual
Quality Improvement. To help achieve this I recommended that they should try and follow the instruction given by Jesus 'In everything, do to others what
you would have them do to you.' Matthew chapter 7
verse 12.

The actual audit took place on 25 January and
we were awarded an average score of 2.6, out of a
possible 3.0, which I was quite pleased with. We
had scored highly on the quality of our teaching
materials and the quality and extent of the services
which we provided for the general public. Both of
these areas gained the highest score given to any
faculty in the University. This surprised many
people, especially the contribution made to society
at large, because everyone naturally assumed that
the Faculty of Humanities, which taught the Social
Sciences, would score highest in this area. The
Unipharm and Unipure projects helped us score
well, but we also had several high profile research
projects and two in public health had gained international funding from the WHO and the Danish
Government, so taken together these made us very
strong in this area. We continued to contribute to the

public good with subsequent projects of national interest, such as later in the year the University Community Pharmacy becoming the only community pharmacy in the country to be officially included in the initial stages of the implementation of the Government's 30 Baht Health Care Policy. The Faculty was beginning to make an impact for good, adding to the overall contribution made by the University and boosting its reputation. Maybe we were getting in tune with the university motto which is officially translated into English as 'Public devotion is a virtue to the learned'. Perhaps this would be understood better as 'Public devotion should be a virtue of the educated'? One does however lose a certain mind teasing charm when trying to improve 'Thinglish'. Take the following 'mission statement'? which is written very elegantly on the wall of the entrance hall of the University of Chiang Mai, Faculty of Pharmacy. 'Excellence in Pharmacy, Quality Focussing, Local Wisdom Development and Self Reliance'. It certainly makes the English visitor think a lot more than 'Excellence in Pharmacy, Focussing on Quality and the Development of Local Wisdom and Self Reliance'.

The main cause of our losing marks in the QA Audit was that our documentation was not as complete as it should have been in some areas especially in the area of financial documentation and records of all communications with the University Finance Department. I had tried hard to understand the faculty finances and had done my best to keep a tight control, but the procedures were not yet good enough. In fact we found out a few months later that two of our administrative staff had been helping themselves to considerable amounts of faculty money. They were both dismissed and I put procedures into place to recover the money. For one of them it was going to take at least 18 months to repay the money.

On St. Valentine's Day we had the tradition of providing several large iced light sponge cakes for a small faculty party. During the party I would say a few words to tell all the staff how much they were appreciated and make the point that it was God's love to us that we were really celebrating. When speaking in the Thai language it is important to get the tones correct or one can say something different from what one had intended. There are five tones, high; medium; low; rising and falling. It is also important to get the vowel sounds not only correct but also of the right length. Vowels can be long or short and the meaning can be quite different for each. At the party mentioned above, in 2001, I startled some of the staff, perhaps more than I originally thought, by using a long vowel instead of a short one in a critical situation. I intended saying that 'our faculty was a poor faculty', 'kana rao pen kana jon' (because we were an autonomous faculty not in receipt of all of the budgets enjoyed by government faculties). I actually said 'our faculty is a faculty of robbers', 'kana rao pen kana joan'! When I apologised and corrected myself one or two said 'Oh, we knew that you did not really mean it', but it struck me that there were one or two relieved looking faces. This illustration also indicates that the name 'Joan' is rather an unfortunate name to have in Thailand. Unless a Thai person knows Joan very well they are not comfortable to use her name. Joan has the Thai name 'Jaroonsri', which was given to her in 1959 during the six weeks we lived in Lopburi undertaking language study before starting full-time medical work, and many people prefer to use this name. If they are not aware of her name 'Jaroonsri' they may prefer to call her 'Mem', 'Jo-Anne', or 'Jones'.

As part of our involvement with the 30 Baht Health Scheme, Dr. Kraisorn, one of our lecturers, arranged that I should speak in May at a seminar on the subject organised by Mr. Pongteb, a lecturer at the Prince of Songkla University in South Thailand. Kraisorn obtained his PhD from the University of Wales and Pongteb had studied a WHO/ RGU course at RGU on 'Essential Drug Management and Rational Drug Use'. The seminar went well but something even more exciting happened when I was in Hadyai. On arrival we were met at Hadyai airport by Pongteb and as we were driving in to town I said to Pongteb, 'Although I have visited the Prince of Songkla University several times already I have not yet been able to meet up with Dr. Krassanai of the Dental Faculty. Do you know how I might contact him?' Pongteb got out his mobile phone and in a minute or two I was talking to Krassanai on the phone and making arrangements to have a meal with him that evening. This was really something because I had heard about Krassanai from Andrew Way over

30 years ago and had seen reference to him from time to time in OMF literature. Now I was going to meet the man I had heard so much about and prayed for over the years. Over the meal and afterwards Krassanai told me the quite thrilling story of how he had come to know the Lord and how the Lord had led him into different avenues of service. Here was someone with experience of; TCS as an influential student leader (see page 174) and later as a key graduate leader and supporter, working at the Christian Hospital Manorom as the first Thai Dentist, undertaking postgraduate study in Belfast, working as a university lecturer and then as Dean of the Dental Faculty at the Prince of Songkla University, holding key committee appointments at both national and international levels, helping establish and lead a thriving Church in Hadyai and also initiating and having a key role in the running of quite a large mainly charitable Dental Clinic. There was so much that I could learn from him and this was an additional unexpected blessing from my visit to South Thailand. We had a lot in common but had never before been in the same place at the same time, but now the Lord had arranged it, as the Chinese Christians in Nanjing and elsewhere always said to me when we met unexpectedly and seemingly by chance. Krassanai was able to tell me about many of the major developments that had taken place in the Christian student work after Joan and I left in August 1969. (He later encouraged me to attend the TCS 33rd Anniversary Thanksgiving Service, 23 October and Camp 24-26 October 2003. Four

hundred students and graduates attended the camp which was a great time of praising the Lord for what he had done and was doing through TCS. There are now 18 TCS staff and 12 Associate TCS staff. I was told several times by different people that TCS had made a major impact on the development and strengthening of the church in all parts of Thailand over the last 30 years. Many former TCS members are now pastors of churches and others hold influential Christian and secular leadership positions.)

Very soon after Kraisorn and I got back to MSU it was time to go off on a faculty conference on 13 June. This conference was so that we could plan faculty policy for the academic year ahead. The conference was to be held at the Golden Valley Resort in Khao Yai (big mountain). This is a National Park area about 200 miles or so south of us and is a very popular holiday area. I had been to a different resort in the same area on a previous occasion to attend a university conference when we discussed whether we would wish to move to being an autonomous university. The majority seemed to be in favour of such a move but the process is taking a very long time and several years later MSU is still a university under government control. (In the Bangkok Post of 22 April 2003, there is a report of a recent meeting of university lecturers that wished to express to the government their opinion that it was better for university education that universities remained in the government sector and were free from the responsibility of generating income). I think that many lecturers prefer to remain as civil servants with all the fringe benefits and status that this gives them.

I had prepared my contributions to the faculty conference scheduled in June before travelling down to Hadyai in May and so felt fairly relaxed about things. After arriving at the resort we were told to watch out for an unusual sight. Just before dusk, at about 6.15 pm, a black cloud could be seen high in the sky and moving at speed down the valley. It was, as we could see when it got closer, thousands of bats heading off to some nightly rendezvous. In my limited experience of such things this seemed to be something quite special.

That evening after supper I felt that I should prepare an extra presentation for the opening session next morning on faculty policy and I stayed up quite late doing this. Next morning, just before I was due to speak; it was found that the hand out material I had prepared for the conference before my visit to Hadyai had been left behind at MSU! If the Lord had not prompted me to prepare extra material the previous evening, which was not absolutely dependent on those hand outs, I would have been left in rather an embarrassing situation. As it was my presentation went very well and provided guidelines for a series of working groups to then develop the details for different aspects of the faculty's work for implementation on our return to MSU. The conference was a great success and all the staff were very happy and enthusiastic. We also had some good fun sessions fitted into the schedule and at the end of the conference every participant wrote me a personal message of encouragement on a set of little blue paper hearts. That was a special Thai touch to proceedings. A less usual Thai characteristic of this conference, its unusualness made it very noticeable and endearing, was that from the moment our bus left MSU to the moment we arrived back, everything ran exactly according to schedule. I had rarely if ever experienced this in Thailand, but the conference organising committee had obviously made it a priority objective and had been successful in achieving it. We were most impressed and very appreciative that they had made this effort especially for us.

CHAPTER 13

THE FINAL PRODUCT

After the good conference in Khao Yai we were fairly confident that the faculty was administratively in fairly good order to function efficiently for the next academic year (June 01 – March 02). The major problem which still remained was the lack of a government budget for our faculty building.

Within six days of returning from the faculty conference on 14 June we had attended the opening of the new church building in Mahasarakham on 17 June and travelled to Chiang Mai on 20 June. This was to attend a special meeting of the Deans of all Faculties of Pharmacy to celebrate the appointment of a pharmacist to the position of President of the University of Chiang Mai. Dr. Nipon was the third pharmacy academic to be appointed as the President of a government university, (following Dr. Pavich at Mahasarakham and Dr. Monthorn at Naresuan), and all three had obtained their PhDs in Britain. Then we did not return to Mahasarakham but on Sunday 24 June we flew from Chiang Mai via Bangkok and Amsterdam to Aberdeen. I needed to be home to support both Nusaraporn and Sunantha who were spending several months in Aberdeen over the summer as part of their PhD studies. Nusaraporn would complete her PhD at the end of this visit, and was therefore involved in writing up, but Sunantha still had another year before she would be finished. Then there was personal medicine to be collected and as many family as possible to be visited. I would also be involved with the second group of PharmD students doing their Introductory Community Pharmacy course at De Montfort University Leicester and their Practice Placements in Lincoln. Initial work on the Third Edition of 'Pharmaceutical Practice', a popular pharmacy textbook, would also be commenced. The responsibilities of co-editing and part-authoring this book were already causing us to think that we needed to have more time in Aberdeen during 2002 in order for me to have the time to do my part in ensuring that this book was ready for the publishers in September 02. We had also arranged to have our house roof completely re-slated during August and then we planned to return to Thailand on 3 September in time to get my yearly contract and work permits organised and our visas renewed before their expiry on 30 September. There were many potential pitfalls with all these arrange-ments needing to dovetail, in order to keep to sched-ule, but in answer to the prayers of many these things all worked out smoothly as planned. Again we were thankful to God for His good hand upon us.

On 4 September after good flights we were back in Thailand and stayed again with Woranoot at the Bangkok Christian College to rest up and then travel on to Mahasarakham two days later. I think I have mentioned before that we needed to take a break, if possible, in Bangkok to get over the journey, as the work started almost immediately on arrival and sometimes on arrival at Khon Kaen before the last lap of the journey commenced. The next day I took part in a research seminar and the day after that Professor David Hughes from the University of Wales, Swansea, visited and I went with him to see our president. David was interested in health systems and was exploring the possibility of spending a sabbatical year with us at Mahasarakham and undertaking research in the area of, 'The implementation problems arising from the introduction of the 30 Baht Government universal health care policy'. In due course this sabbatical arrangement worked out and David commenced his visit about a year later. There were other spin offs from David working a year at MSU such as Songkramchai was accepted for a University PhD with David. This was a very satisfactory development, when it occurred, because I had suggested long before David actually was directly involved with the faculty that Songkramchai should seek to undertake a PhD with him. Songkramchai had other ideas and at first wanted to go to Australia and then actually visited Leeds for several weeks to try and get accepted there but I think there were problems with his English. Eventually he saw sense and realised that he was very fortunate to have such a good opportunity as was still being offered him to work with David and he started that cooperation while David was at MSU.

Another development which was proceeding rather slowly was the development of the five track Masters in Public Health curriculum and I needed to give a supportive hand to those developments because we were aiming to take our first intake of 60 or so graduates in June 2002. The curriculum for the first bachelor degree in Thai Traditional Medicine was also being progressed. The President was keen to have this degree established as soon as possible and facilitated the establishment of two lectureships in this area so that we were able to quickly appoint two extra staff with relevant expertise to support our existing staff in developing this new venture.

Dealing with all the paperwork and electronic communications that were always awaiting me when I returned was also something that I liked to deal with as soon as possible. Then there was the immediate round of meetings that I was obliged to attend. The proliferation of meetings seemed to me to have become something of a high status activity that was pursued with vigour by many Thai academics.

The following week six of the first group of PharmD students were due at the university to deliver the oral presentations, in Thai, of their research projects and I was involved. It is quite a demanding exercise to listen, question and assess this type of oral presentation appropriately for the quality of both presentation and content.

Before Joan and I had time to think about settling in we were already slotted back into life at Mahasarakham, but we were also aware that we needed to plan and prepare the faculty as well as we could to function without us in the not too distant future.

From the above it seems that the faculty was running quite well with no problems and of course this would be too good to be true. There were inevitably some problems even when things were in general going well. For example a slightly more senior member of staff had recently joined us who had more academic experience than many of our staff and also a lot of ideas, energy and drive to try and implement them. I believe it would be true to say that he almost automatically expected to have his way in everything and did not feel it necessary to find out if there was an accepted policy in a particular situation and to seek to implement that policy. Needless to say this resulted in some disruption and friction, but fortunately there was at least one area of responsibility which needed his energy and experience and where he made a very useful contribution. A better contribution than any of the others could make at that time.

Then on 11 September, as we were sitting watching a live CNN broadcast, we came face to face on our television screen with the coordinated terrorist attack on America which changed the world. International travel, the safety of expatriates and tourists and the way governments treat security matters have all been affected dramatically. We noticed the impact immediately. As the result of fairly long term planning, together with Professor Ed. Moreton of the University of Maryland, we had one of their recent PharmD graduates come to MSU, to work with us for six months, to help us upgrade the clinical pharmacy practice in Mahasarakham hospital. Janine had only been with us a few weeks and we were appreciating her contribution, but within ten days of the attack on America she was on her way home because of fears for security. I believe that it is important to accept the decision of the individual in these circumstances, even though I personally felt that there was little or no increased risk to her or us at that time. No one could say categorically that it was safe however, and so if the person felt unsafe and their family felt they were unsafe then it was better for them to leave. About six weeks later two of our first group of MSU PharmD students, Wilawan and Phayom who had just completed their PharmD coursework, were due to go to the University of Maryland under Ed. Moreton's jurisdiction, for two to three months clinical pharmacy experience. I strongly advised these two to go, even though America was a potentially more dangerous place than Mahasarakham at that time. The benefits to risks ratio for Wilawan and Phayom were, I believe, heavily weighted in favour of their going. They agreed and so these two went to America and benefited greatly from their experience. Both had previously been to Aberdeen for five weeks and the additional experience in America was not only professionally beneficial, but also a maturing experience for them and fulfilled the objective of adding to the expertise available at MSU.

On Thursday 27 September the Deputy Minister of Health spoke at Mahasarakham to the Provincial Health Workers on the 30 Baht health care policy, but no mention was made of the participation of community pharmacists. It would be a very serious matter if the contribution of Community Pharmacy was left out of the government's implementation of such a major healthcare reform. At the coffee break I was given a special opportunity, together with Dr. Chai,the Medical Director of Mahasarakham Hospital, to speak to the minister on this matter. I was able to tell him of our plans to have the University Community Pharmacy undertake a major research project to explore the various ways community pharmacy could contribute to the 30 Baht healthcare provision. The minister gave us encouragement to go ahead with these plans. It so happened that the very next day we had arranged for our Community Pharmacy premises and the practice of our pharmacists to be officially assessed by the top officials of the Community Pharmacy Association of Thailand. This was with the object of receiving validation as a pharmacy which had facilities and staff of a standard necessary for providing good quality pharmaceutical care to the local community. This was duly achieved. We then went to the hospital and signed a contract with Dr. Chai for cooperation between the Provincial Hospital staff and the University Community Pharmacy staff to undertake research into areas in which the pharmacists in the University Community Pharmacy could cooperate with the hospital staff on the implementation of the 30 Baht healthcare project. Subsequently we were successful, against open competition from other universities and organisations, in obtaining funding for several major research projects. These were to: i) evaluate the healthcare needs of the community in the area served by the University Pharmacy; ii) investigate the role of the pharmacist in treating chronic and long-term illnesses, specifically, diabetes, hypertension and pulmonary tuberculosis; iii) investigate the role of the pharmacist in treating common illnesses; iv) investigate the role of the pharmacist in health promotion.

Ours was the only community pharmacy in Thailand which became an official part of the research into the implementation of the government's 30 Baht healthcare scheme.

In October I wrote a letter to the President of the University, Dr. Pavich, informing him that I wished to stand down from being Dean of the Faculty as from March 2002, but that I would be prepared to continue with other university responsibilities until the end of my contract in September. This was, as mentioned previously, because of my commitments with writing and editing the book 'Pharmaceutical Practice' and because of responsibilities supervising the write-up of Sunantha's PhD thesis in Aberdeen, May-August 2002. I did not get a reply but I assumed that this had been taken note of and accepted. It was not until 6 February 2002 that I had the opportunity of discussing the future of the faculty with Pavich and in the course of discussion I asked him what his plans were with regards to the appointment of a new Dean. Pavich said that he had done nothing about it and he asked me what my suggestions were. In fact until fairly recently I had assumed that Sunantha would be the next Dean when she completed her PhD in the summer/autumn of 2002. Although Sunantha had said on several occasions that she did not want to be Dean when I left, I had thought that this was just a modest or polite answer with the intention of making me feel still wanted and that when the time came then she would be prepared to be Dean. However, in recent discussions Sunantha had convinced me that she did not want to be Dean, so I said to Pavich that I thought it would have to be someone from another university, but that I would check it once more with Sunantha. If Sunantha still said, 'No.' then I suggested that Aroonsri of the University of Khon Kaen might be a possibility, because she already had experience of being a Deputy Dean in the Faculty of Pharmaceutical Sciences there and had also acted as an assistant to Dr. Bungorn, the first Dean of the Faculty of Pharmacy at the University of Ubonrachathani. Aroonsri had studied for her PhD at RGU with me as one of her supervisors. This had the disadvantage that it made it culturally very difficult for Aroonsri to say 'No.' but in the event this did not prove to be a difficulty because she independently believed that God would have her take this position when I left. That is how it eventually took place. At the first meeting of the newly constituted Faculty Board on 6 April the decision was made to propose to the University Council meeting of 18 April that Aroonsri was appointed Dean as from 1 May and that I would step down as Dean as from 30 April. It was hard for us to make the decision to let go but we knew that we must and we had been enabled to do it. We were very grateful to the Lord for all that He had done to enable us both to dispense the 'Mahasarakham Prescription' and we trusted that 'The Final Product' would prove to be very efficacious and have an indefinite shelf life. However, my contract did not expire until 30 September and we thought that we would have another spell at MSU in order to complete my responsibilities there once Sunantha had completed her PhD and all the work on the book had been completed. In the event Aroonsri emailed us that the Council of MSU had decided at their July meeting that they would offer me an honorary doctorate which if accepted would be conferred by HRH Princess Maha Chakri Sirindhorn at the December graduation ceremony. In the light of that decision we were advised to delay our next visit to MSU until December.

Sunantha successfully defended her PhD at her oral on 1 August and the completed manuscript for the third edition of 'Pharmaceutical Practice' was delivered on time to the publishers in Edinburgh on 30 September by Arthur Winfield. So we were then free to get on with other things and prepare for our next visit to Thailand in December.

CHAPTER 14

A PLEASANT AFTERTASTE

On Tuesday 3 December 2002 we returned to MSU for the Graduation Ceremony and to visit Chiang Mai University (CMU) Faculty of Pharmacy. The latter was for discussions on the progress of the seven universities Consortium PhD Project and on the progress of Phayom's PhD studies which were part of the project. As was our usual custom we committed it all to God asking for His guidance and overruling. We also entrusted ourselves to Him to keep us fit and to enable us through all the stresses caused by international travel, changes of language, time, climate, food and daily routine and to help us to be able to adapt, be patient and flexible when and where necessary. In addition we looked to God to overrule so that we would be able to meet the relevant people that we felt it would be helpful and useful to meet up with on this visit. Many friends around the UK and in our local church Gilcomston South Church of Scotland, together with our family, supported us in prayer throughout this visit.

Tom Scott delivered us to Dyce airport, Aberdeen, in good time for our KLM UK 3.40 pm plane to Amsterdam to connect with the 7.40 pm onward KLM flight to Bangkok. On attempting to check in for the Amsterdam flight we were somewhat startled to be told that our flight was five hours late and therefore it would not get to Amsterdam in time to make the flight connection to Bangkok. We were directed to another desk where we joined the queue to renegotiate our travel plans. After some silent prayer and a little discussion it was agreed that we should take the next British Airways flight to London, Heathrow, and then the 10.00 pm Quantas flight to Bangkok. Although we would arrive in Bangkok four hours later than planned we would still be able to keep to our original schedule. The rearranged flights worked out well and we arrived in Bangkok quite well rested even though the business class seats were not of the best design. Neither was the food of particularly good quality, but we were grateful to arrive safely on time and in good order.

For approximately two years now we have travelled business class on the Amsterdam to Bangkok leg of the flight because we find that we arrive in much better condition and recover more quickly from the journey. We also take half an aspirin tablet daily for two days before travel to reduce the possibility of the initiation of blood clots due to inactivity and dehydration on the flight. In addition we try to reduce our caffeine and fatty food intake for 24 hours or so before flying. On the plane we don't partake of alcohol but try to keep up a good intake of water and we exercise our ankles and calves at intervals during the flight. These various procedures are probably especially helpful for the elderly, such as ourselves, to follow.

The arrival time of 4.00 pm local time proved to be very convenient and instead of the frequently experienced queuing and delays for up to one hour we passed straight through immigration without delay.

Naeti, a recent PhD of RGU and a lecturer in the Faculty of Pharmacy, Mahidol University, Bangkok, was expecting to meet us at 11.20 am. We tried to let him know that we would be late. From Heathrow we contacted our daughter Megan by phone and asked her to email Sunantha at Mahasarakham telling her of the delay and asking her to contact Naeti in Bangkok by phone informing him of our revised travel plans. The message reached him too late to prevent him meeting our original flight. However, he was at the airport to meet us having obtained our revised travel arrangements from KLM in Bangkok when he realised that we were not on our original flight. After meeting Naeti I booked two seats on the Friday mid-morning flight to Khon Kaen. Now we could relax.

Naeti drove us through some rather congested traffic to the Narai Hotel, in Silom Road, where we quickly settled in as we were quite familiar with the place.

Thursday 5 December was the King of Thailand's (and my) birthday so it was a public holiday. We walked the short distance to the Central department store and bought one or two pieces of cutlery for our time in MSU. This was the first department store to be built in Bangkok. About 4.00 pm, after a short rest, we took a taxi to the Oriental Hotel and had a fruit cocktail on the terrace overlooking the River Chao Phrya, followed by some Thai food and ice cream - a very enjoyable 70th birthday celebration. A surprise was still to come because when we were back in our hotel room at 9.00 pm Megan phoned to wish me a Happy Birthday!

The next morning at 9.00 am we took a hotel car to the airport and flew to Khon Kaen where we were met at the airport by Nusaraporn with a Khon Kaen University mini-bus and driver to transfer us to the Sofitel for the weekend. After a rest we had discussions at 3.30 pm with Aroonsri who also told us that Pastor Nipon of the Khon Kaen Chinese Church, would like us both to give a word of testimony at the Sunday morning service. In the evening a group of Khon Kaen lecturers, who were alumni of RGU, took us out for a meal.

On Saturday evening we had a very pleasant meal with Supatra, Wittya her surgeon husband and their youngest two children – June and Jade – Gem the eldest was at school in Bangkok preparing for university entrance examinations. Supatra's father had died since we saw them last but this sad news had not yet been told to her mother who was living with another one of her daughters in Bangkok.

Sommai and Aroonsri with their teenage son Ming took us to church on Sunday morning. We have had an association with the Khon Kaen Chinese Church for about 18 of its 21 years existence. After the church service we were presented with a clock in a glass frame which also contained a wooden cross on a background of locally made patterned cotton. We stayed to have communal lunch with the church members as is their custom each Sunday. In the evening Wiwat, his wife Tarani, his mother and niece took us out to a meal. His mother had actually visited us in Aberdeen at the time Wiwat was completing his studies there and she was very pleased to see us again.

Monday morning Chaiyagarn collected us in the Faculty vehicle, an Isuzu 4x4. The familiar routine of our return to MSU was followed. This consisted of calling in at the Tesco Lotus supermarket for breakfast provisions for our time at MSU and stopping for bananas at a roadside stall about 10 miles outside Khon Kaen. Sunantha was waiting to welcome us at the MSU Condominium Number 1. The friendly guard and Chaiyagarn quickly rallied round to help move our luggage to the lift and then to our old flat on the eighth floor. I was then given the keys to the Mitsubishi Lancer car that I had used before. We then went off to lunch with Sunantha in the new student canteen. This was a great improvement on the previous three canteens. Then we were shown round the new student Shopping Plaza where the second university pharmacy was now located. About 5000 students lived in Halls of residence in

this area. Afterwards we returned to the condominium. In the evening Sunantha and Phayom took
us to the Silver Plate restaurant which is our
favourite restaurant in Mahasarakham. It belongs to
the President of the University's younger sister and
had opened about 18 months previously.

Tuesday 10 December I went to my old office
that was all set up for me and after accessing my
emails I had two and a half hours of discussions with
Phayom about her research. Naeti and Nusaraporn
also arrived to spend a few days helping Sunantha
with the translation into Thai of the second edition
of 'Pharmaceutical Practice'. (Actually some 16
RGU alumni who were now lecturers at various Thai
universities were combining forces to translate this
book.) We all had lunch together under the thatched
roofed, open sided, Golden Bamboo Bush restaurant
which was located by the side of fish cultivation
ponds. In the evening Joan and I were back at the
Silver Plate for another meal. Afterwards we called
in at the University Pharmacy located near the night
market. The pharmacy stays open until 10.00pm and
like the one on the university campus is staffed by a
pharmacist manager and by pharmacists who are
university lecturers working to a rota.

Both Joan and I worked in the office on
Wednesday morning and talked with some of the
lecturers. In the early afternoon we had an hour with
Dr. Pavich, the President of the University. Then I
tried to arrange for the purchase of air tickets from
Khon Kaen via Bangkok to Chiang Mai on 20
December. It was difficult to get tickets and we had to

opt for business class in order to get a booking. I also found that all the flights from Chiang Mai to Bangkok on 2 January 2003 were already fully booked. We were put on the waiting list for business class tickets. Our international flights from Bangkok to Amsterdam were 11.25 pm on 2 January. An emailed prayer request went to Dominic Smart at Gilcomston for the church Saturday evening prayer meeting and we kept Megan informed by our regular emails.

In the morning of 12 December I went with Sunantha to look round the Drinking Water manufacturing facility, which now had 9 full-time workers. The chief hold-up to further expansion was shortage of water for much of the year. Nevertheless the facility was now producing, distributing and selling sufficient drinking water to bring in a healthy monthly profit. We also walked round the recently completed medicines manufacturing plant which had been built next to the drinking water plant so that it would have an accessible potable water supply. This would soon be another facility providing medicines, including herbal remedies, for local people. The manufacturing will be combined with undergraduate teaching and the facility will have research laboratories.

It was planned that we should eat our lunch with the Deans of all the 12 University Faculties of Pharmacy, who had arranged to hold their monthly meeting at Mahasarakham, so that they could attend the special celebration organised by the MSU Faculty for my honorary doctorate. The lunch meal and their meeting were to be in the President's central administration building. We were a little concerned because a meeting of all university presidents and all university deans had been hastily arranged in Bangkok and our president who was chairman of that committee was obliged to attend that meeting. Were the pharmacy deans going to attend the Bangkok meeting or were they going to keep their original commitment and come to MSU? They came to MSU.

The Faculty celebration commenced at 5.30 pm. A lot of work had been put into decorating the large open area of the second floor of the triangular building where the Faculty of Pharmacy and Health Sciences was temporarily located. A Thai classical orchestra (Thai musical instruments) and Thai classical dancers from the University Fine Arts Department took part. Across the back of the stage were these words, "With love and heart felt pride to Professor R.M.E. Richards, OBE". A booklet had been prepared giving some of my academic and professional details and information about the development of the Faculty and a power point presentation was shown using photographs of my time at MSU. Speeches were made. Photographs were taken. Numerous large baskets and bouquets of flowers were presented, together with individual presents from staff, former and present students, presents from the other faculties within the university and from all the 12 Faculties of Pharmacy throughout Thailand. Thirteen of the 15 Thai PhDs during my time at RGU attended. They all brought their academic gowns and we were photographed together. Representatives of the NE Thailand Pharmacists Association were there and various people from Public Health Centres. We were especially delighted that Professor Malyn was present at the celebration. Malyn is one of only four Thai pharmacy academics who are full professors in pharmacy. We had known her from her student days at Chula when she attended the student Bible studies. Over the years Malyn had kept in touch with us whenever possible when we visited Thailand. Malyn had invited me to lecture at Mahidol University, taken us out to meals, discussed research, attended my Honorary Doctorate celebrations at Khon Kaen University and spent several months doing research with me in Aberdeen. In addition Malyn has offered to help with developments in the Faculty of Pharmacy and Health Sciences at MSU.

In personal conversation I was quite surprised to hear that the Pharmacy Deans from both Chulalongkorn and Mahidol Universities in Bangkok remembered me teaching them at Chulalongkorn in 1967 when it was the only Faculty of Pharmacy that was graduating pharmacists in Thailand. This was the same time as the President of MSU was undertaking his pharmacy studies at Chula. (Chiang Mai Faculty of Pharmacy had been receiving students for about two years but none had completed their course at that time.)

This was a wonderful evening and Joan and I were flattered and thrilled and almost overwhelmed with all the loving friendliness, generosity, good wishes and kindness that were showered upon us, but this was only the beginning. The actual graduation was not until the following Tuesday!

Friday was a quiet day by comparison. Quite a lot of it was spent trying to contact Dr. Chai the Director of Mahasarakham General Hospital and a fellow advisor for Phayom's PhD studies, but he proved to be very busy. In fact he was just about to move to be director of a larger hospital, in another provincial capital, and was running out of time to do all the things that were being lined up for him.

Saturday, on the other hand, was a day in which we accomplished rather more than we had expected. For several years Sunantha had been encouraging us to visit the site of the excavated remains of dinosaurs that had been found a few years before in the adjoining province of Kalasin. Joan and I had set out in our car on a previous occasion but had turned back before we had reached the site. Now a museum had been developed over the main cluster of skeletal remains and MSU researchers from France were involved in developing the project. Sunantha drove the Faculty vehicle and Kusama and Wanida, two lady lecturers, also joined the expedition. It was a very interesting visit and the first such dinosaur site that I had seen but I felt that the exhibits and supporting materials left rather a lot to the imagination.

After lunch in Kalasin we headed for Roi Et. This was specifically to see Mr. Teerawut. When we last visited him his wife was expecting their third child about June 2002. We wanted to see their child and to encourage Teerawut with his studies. You will remember he was one of the first group of pharmacists who enrolled for the two year PharmD course in June 1999. On this visit to his pharmacy we found him to be in very good spirits and very pleased with the addition of his now six month old son to his six and four year old daughters. Although his illness has delayed him he has nevertheless progressed with his studies and should complete them in 2003. After leaving Teerawut and family we headed for Wilawan, back in the centre of Mahasarakham town. She was also in the first group of PharmD students and having completed the degree was now a lecturer. At that time however, she was on maternity leave having had her baby boy just a few weeks before.

In the evening we attended a celebratory dinner for the 225 public health workers who would receive their Bachelor of Public Health (BPH) degrees on the following Tuesday. During the early evening I was told that I would be required to be present early the next morning dressed in my gown to have photographs taken. The taking of the photographs would be at a time which was impossible to specify exactly. They would be group photographs taken together with those graduating PharmD and BPH. Our plans to attend church were modified accordingly. Phayom would take Joan and Aroonsri and I would follow on after the photographs had been taken. Joan got a very warm welcome by the people at church. Aroonsri and I arrived during the Bible study just before the service started and all were very pleased to see us. Aroonsri had to hurry away after the service but the rest of us stayed for the communal meal which also provided time for friendly chat and catching up with news. We heard that there had been five baptisms in the time we had been away. There was also harvest of another kind in that the paddy field next to the church, which the church had rented, yielded a bumper crop of long grained fragrant rice and sticky rice. Both types were packed into sacks and stored in the church library! Hopefully it was a temporary measure. All too soon we were on our way again.

In the evening Methin, who was by this time about two thirds of the way through his studies for a PhD at Mahidol University, took us out for a meal. When we arrived at MSU the total English conversation Methin could muster was 'Good morning! How are you?' He would then produce beads of sweat on his brow thinking how to proceed! Now he could carry on the whole conversation in English while we ate together. He had made better use of the opportunity to study English conversation with us in our first two years at MSU than most staff.

On Monday morning I had a discussion with Juntip on her PhD research. Then the celebratory lunch for the seven pharmacists graduating PharmD was held in the restaurant of Condominium 1. This restaurant had been functioning about one year and had developed into a very useful additional facility. Students from each of the first three years of the six year undergraduate PharmD programme were present. Each of those graduating, including me, were expected to sing a least one song from the computerised Karaoke set-up and make a little speech. I, helped by Joan, sang the carol 'Silent

Night' and explained briefly the Christmas story. All of the PharmDs spoke of how the course they had just completed had given them more skills and abilities to practise as pharmacists. Wiraporn, was especially enthusiastic about all the things she could do in her work as a hospital pharmacist which she could not do before. Her husband, a doctor, had worked at a Baptist hospital. He was in the process of completing his training to be a surgeon and was living temporarily in Bangkok. The plan is that when he qualifies as a surgeon they will set up a home of their own. Wiraporn then plans to be baptised. At present she is living with her parents who are not Christians and is delaying her baptism in deference to them. This is an example of how the Thai in general are very considerate about the feelings of their elders and try very hard not to go against their wishes in a given situation, even when they themselves would like to do something different from what their elders might prefer. Wiraporn's deference to her parent's in this matter of delaying her baptism is an example of being 'greng jai', which is a deeply felt concept in Thai society and governs attitudes and relationships between one person and another. Therefore, I would like to try and give an insight into the meaning of this term, because the influence of greng jai on the Thais' attitudes must be appreciated in order to help understand what is happening and influencing behaviour in particular face to face situations.

The Thais have an automatic feeling of greng jai but the foreigner does not have this and therefore it is necessary that she/he makes an effort to understand or get a feel of the concept. The words greng jai are not easily translatable into English. Literally greng jai is 'fear heart', which in practise is an attitude of respectful fear. In the foregoing description in connection with Wiraporn and her parents I have used 'considerate' and 'deference'. But of course it is necessary to know who is expected to be in respectful fear, of whom, in order to show the necessary consideration automatically expected. The overruling concept in Thai society, which will help unlock this underlying theme or custom, is respect for one's elders, and the obedience to one's elders and their superior wisdom which is automatically assumed. This is where the modern foreigner might have a different set of values and must be ready to make radical adjustments in their thinking and check their behaviour or they may unwittingly cause offence and give the impression of being impolite and uneducated. Respect for one's elders is a general rule, but this applies particularly within the family where, parents, grandparents and older relatives are all held in respectful fear and deferred to. In the work situation respect for elders and respect for a person's position in the hierarchal structure will take precedence to respect for higher qualifications, which may be held by a younger person. It may be that a younger person can see clearly that a particular course of action needs urgent implementation, but it is very unlikely that they will feel able to suggest this to their elders in the workplace, without being first asked. This again may be a situation where the foreigner might need to make adjustments in their attitudes and practises. It can certainly cause frustrations, not only to foreigners, but also to many Thai returning from overseas with high qualifications when they are not given the opportunity and freedom which they might wish to use those qualifications. I have noticed however that if they are prepared to be a little patient and not act in a proud way then the opportunities often follow.

In addition to the general rule of respect for one's elders it is also helpful to the understanding of greng jai to appreciate that the smooth operation of Thai society depends a great deal on having good relationships with people who hold power in government institutions, which are very bureaucratic. Those who know people in the right places are themselves able to wield more power and this not only helps them in getting things done but it also means that others need to be greng jai of them. This is particularly so if they are wanting help from the person with connections in getting a particular thing done. Unfortunately this can have the consequences that are not desirable. That is in attempts to be seen to be showing proper respect, gifts and favours are given, and a certain amount of flattery and fawning may take place.

It should also be said that a very important aspect of being greng jai involves the avoidance of any kind of confrontation which would imply disagreement with one's elder, or superior. Confrontation would most likely be interpreted as disrespect and cause offence, so it would be unlikely to result in an outcome that was beneficial to the one in the less powerful position. The avoidance of confrontation also leads to indirectness and diffidence in language and behaviour so that a foreigner, in particular, may draw completely wrong conclusions from a particular meeting or discussion with others. I was disappointed many times, during my first years in Thailand, when I had invited someone to come to a meeting and they replied, 'I would like to come', but then on the day they did not come. It later became clear to me that there were many ways to respond to an invitation. All the responses sounded friendly, polite and encouraging, in order to please the hearer, but some in fact meant that they would not come, others meant that there was a fifty-fifty chance they would come and others meant that they would definitely come.

Another aspect of greng jai is self-effacement, or depreciation of oneself, almost to becoming an invisible or a non person. It is well to be aware that the person who is hiding his light under a bushel may be highly capable and should not be passed over, or dismissed from one's plans, without exploring much more closely what his actual abilities are for a particular task. The fact that such a person did not speak up in a particular situation cannot be automatically assumed to be lack of interest, commitment or ability.

I hope these comments might be useful and helpful to any reader who may at some stage undertake work in Thailand. These things should also be born in mind by those who make friends with Thai students or maybe students from some other Asian countries.

The next day was graduation day and from first light the campus was humming with activity. More like Piccadilly Circus than rural Thailand. Several police manned every intersection, whistles were blown vigorously to direct the drivers and to guide them to parking places away from the gymnasium – the place of the graduation. The building is named 'The Completion (or more literally 'Fruit') of Studies Building'. There were approximately 4000 students graduating this year and each had family present. The whole area around the gymnasium was like a big open air market with stalls selling all kinds of things. Police, soldiers and court officials probably accounted for another 2000 or so people. Noise and congestion was unavoidable but everyone was in good spirits and many of the former and current students and families were celebrating excitedly. Bunches of flowers and single red roses were a must for every graduate both male and female.

The restaurant of Condominium Number 1 was the gathering point for the University Council members and for the extra special lunch provided for them, the three of us receiving Honorary Doctorates and the four receiving University Prizes. Actually there were five Honorary Doctorates being awarded. One was awarded to the King. This would be awarded privately and one to HRH Princess Maha Chakri Sirindhorn, which would be awarded at the opening of the Graduation Ceremony by the Chairman of the Council, Mr. Meechai.

It was very convenient for us in the eighth floor flat to be able to rest up for part of the morning and then descend at 11.00 am for lunch with the others. Vice-president Yuwadee, who was also Secretary to the Council, and who was responsible for making sure all arrangements for the Council proceeded as planned, invited us to have lunch at her table. Miss Yuwadee was always most helpful in putting us at ease on such occasions. We decided that this was not the time to overeat but we did share a tempting ice-cream cake between us.

At about 11.45 am we were ferried from the condominium to the gymnasium, about half a mile away, in university mini-buses. This was the only way to move around the campus while it was under the security restrictions. We were ushered to air-conditioned rooms at the back of the gymnasium and those of us involved in the ceremony got changed into our robes which rather puzzlingly for a hot country like Thailand were heavy and hot. Then those of us who were to receive awards from the Princess went to the platform or stage at the front of the gymnasium for a rehearsal. The students, on the other hand, together with those who read out their names, had spent days going through the routine. With so many graduating it was important that the whole procedure was as smooth as possible. The objective was to have a minimum of 27 students per minute receive their awards. In actual fact I understand that 30 students per minute was the number achieved. This was considered highly commendable by the court officials. It's interesting to know the things that contribute to making a successful graduation ceremony!

In the event Aroonsri did brilliantly with the reading of the 225 names for the recipients of the Bachelor of Public health, which was the largest number of people receiving a particular degree.

News reached us in the robing room that the Princess was going to arrive ahead of time so we all quickly got to our seats. The procedure went something like this. As the Princess entered she walked over to the right of the stage, as the audience looked at it, and knelt before the Buddhist altar and then waied to the Buddha image with her hands together and raised to her forehead and her head bowed over towards a cushion which her hands would briefly rest on. This would be repeated two or three times. Candles were then lit. Behind and to the audience's right side of the altar sat five Buddhist monks with crossed legs and facing into the centre of the stage. They intoned prayers throughout the ceremony. On the floor in front of the stage was an elaborate display of flowers. At either side on the floor in front of the stage a soldier in dress uniform was stationed on guard standing at attention, his weapon with bayonet fixed. They held that position with hardly a flicker of a movement for one and a half hours before being replaced by a second pair of ceremonial guards for the second half of the ceremony. The Princess sat on a raised throne like chair in the middle of the stage and towards the front. Behind her were various court officials and police and army officers coordinating security. Immediately in front of the Princess was what might best be described as a lectern on which she rested the degree certificate protected in a hard folder covered with grey Thai silk (the university colours are grey and yellow) and the recipient received it standing in front and on the other side of the lectern. The certificates were passed from the back left of the stage along a row of staff sitting crossed legged on the floor to what was the Princess' right hand side. There would be a continuous stream of students moving methodically down the left of the hall and across the front of the stage from the right of the Princess. As a graduate came opposite the Princess they would pause, turn and face her and bow or curtsey as was appropriate. Almost simultaneously their name would be called and they would take five paces forward and offer their right hand to receive the certificate, but as they did so they would flick their hand smartly upwards from the wrist while opening the palm to show that nothing sinister was concealed in their hand. On receiving their certificate they would back five paces diagonally away and to their right, bow or curtsey then turn right and walk off the platform with the certificate held flat on their chest for all to see. We three honorary doctorates received our awards at the beginning of the ceremony and I was the second in line. As I walked towards the Princess she gave me a friendly smile but I am afraid that I was concentrating so hard to try and ensure that I did the right thing that I gave rather a subdued smile. That evening, the part of the ceremony where I received the degree was shown on all four television channels, but we did not get a chance to see it. Nevertheless, wherever we went after that I was told 'We saw you on television getting your degree from the Princess'.

At the end of the ceremony all the students, who had studied for their degrees at the university, stood and recited in unison after a lecturer their promises to the King, their country, the university, their former lecturers and their religion. Those who received honorary awards did not participate in this.

After the ceremony I was requested to go up to the second floor behind the stage with the University Council members and wait for the Princess to change and prepare herself to travel. When she emerged from her changing room she walked across to one of the council and had a brief conversation about the heat and the environment in general (it was supposed to be the cool season but in fact was quite hot and the MSU gowns were very hot) then she moved along and spoke to another council member who was a jazz musician (like her father, the King) and spoke to him about music. A few more paces and she was opposite me and after eyeing me pensively she asked in English, 'Do you teach here?' I replied, 'I taught here for four and a half years but now I have returned to Aberdeen.' 'Oh, I've visited Aberdeen,' she replied. 'Yes I remember it well,' I said. The Princess smiled broadly and moved away down the stairs to be transported in her cavalcade to a Government rest house at a dam twenty miles north of Khon Kaen. On Thursday 19 December she would officiate at the Khon Kaen University Graduation.

Before dispersing I had my photograph taken with Mr. Meechai and Dr Pavich and then went back to the robing room to disrobe and together with Joan to move to where our transport was waiting. I carried my academic gown over my arm and my Honorary Doctorate Certificate in my hand. As we jostled through the crowd the male and female leaders of the pharmacy undergraduate students congratulated me and gave me heart shaped small cushion like favours attached to sticks about 18 inches long. With these we got into our minibus and were transported to our accommodation. On reaching the flat and putting down the things I was carrying I realised that I no longer had the degree certificate. A little embarrassing to have lost it so soon! Joan and I had a short prayer together. It's very useful having a wife as a prayer partner. I retraced my steps downstairs, but did not find the certificate, so a little sheepishly I asked the guard if he had seen anything. Unfortunately not, so I asked him if he knew the driver who had brought us back, but again drew a blank. He said he would try and find out who the driver was and get him to search his minibus to see if I had dropped the certificate inside. That was now our best hope. I also phoned Aroonsri who said she knew which driver it was who had collected us and she would contact him as soon as possible. About half an hour later a smiling guard appeared at our flat door. He said that the driver had found the certificate in his van and it would be waiting for me at the Faculty of Nursing where the evening University Celebrations for the recipients of Honorary Doctorates were to be held. Another answered prayer by our gracious God. The evening function commenced about 6.00 pm, so we had about half an hour to change and get ourselves ready.

I did not know what to expect at this evening event, but I did know that all Honorary Doctorates were required to make a formal speech, so I was well prepared for this. The Nursing Faculty building was built as a square with an open centre which proved ideal for open air functions, especially in the evening. This time the University Orchestra provided the musical entertainment and the classical Thai dancers and some vocal soloists also took part. The conductor of the orchestra had previously been with the Thai Navy Orchestra and had helped produce a University Orchestra of high standard. On display to the side of the eating area were posters, each with a large photograph and descriptive text giving relevant information about each of us who had received awards. We were all presented with a very large framed photograph of ourselves during the evening. After the meal Mr. Meechai made a speech. He had composed an Ode in the Thai language celebrating the occasion which he recited and afterwards gave us each personal copies. Then each of the recipients of the honours and awards made a short speech. The mood then became somewhat lighter and three of those present who were musicians and songwriters sang one of their own compositions. Dr. Pavich followed with some English songs. At this stage I felt we should make our exit as graciously as possible before someone thought was a good idea for me to sing! The Thai, however, are very accepting and non critical on these occasions and they are very comfortable about performing in public, and perhaps that is why.

We needed to sleep well that night because there had been a change of plan. Instead of having two days of a more relaxing nature with time to catch up on some of the things we had not yet done, such as see Dr. Chai, we were invited to go to Khon Kaen on Wednesday. This was to take part in the celebrations of the Faculty of Pharmacy for an American professor who was to receive an Honorary Doctorate of Khon Kaen University on the Thursday. In fact I was to make a speech congratulating Professor Janet Engle on her award and I was asked to emphasize to Janet how very highly the Honorary Doctorate was regarded by Thai society. It was also suggested that I might mention how I coped with some of the surprises and frustrations that occurred when working in Thailand. For the latter I mentioned patience, perseverance, prayer and flexibility as things I found essential, especially prayer. Janet was certainly an unusual lady. Her academic achievements were impressive and she had helped many Thai students with their studies in America and had visited Thailand to give lectures on several occasions over the last 10 years. To me the really amazing thing was that she had left a 12 week old baby whom she was breast feeding, in charge of her husband in Chicago, in order to collect her award. That must have taken some determination, organisation and persuasive skills. Janet arrived in Thailand on Wednesday, received her degree on Thursday morning and flew back to Chicago on Thursday night. Father and son must have been sure pleased to see her!

Instead of attending the Khon Kaen graduation ceremony I took the opportunity to visit the Thai Airways office to discuss our flights to Chiang Mai via Bangkok on Friday and from Chiang Mai to Bangkok on 2 January. These latter flights needed to be in time to catch our international flight to Amsterdam and so on to Aberdeen. To begin with I could not progress beyond the situation of being told 'All the flights from Chiang Mai to Bangkok on 2 January are full and there is nothing we can do about it other than to put you on the waiting list which we have already done. It is the same every New Year. There are more people who want to fly than there are seats available'. My position was that we needed to catch the KLM 11.25pm flight on 2 January and it was their responsibility to work out a way for us to do this, especially as Joan and I had frequent flyer status with Thai Airways and we had already paid the business class fares but had not been issued with tickets, not even for the Friday flights. The fact that we had an international flight to catch was eventually conceded as being a more critical situation than someone just flying to Bangkok for whom a delay of a day would not be so disastrous. A special phone call was put through to Bangkok asking if someone would make a thorough check of the flight availability on 2 January. I was asked to return in the late afternoon. This I did only to find that the position had not altered but as I was talking to them it was flashed up on the computer screen that a seat had been found and reserved for Joan. I thought that this was an encouragement that God was working and that I would also eventually get a seat. In the mean time it was decided to book flights for both of us on 30 December and also issue tickets for both of us on 2 January. If I got a booking on the 2 January flight before 30 December then I would cancel the December bookings, but if I didn't then we would accept the 30 December flights and cancel Joan's 2 January flight. Under pressure and in God's goodness they had come up with a workable solution and I was pleased with the results of their efforts.

Lunchtime Thursday we were looked after by Drs. Jinda and Jomjai together with Jomjai's husband who was home on holiday from Japan where he was studying for a PhD. We ate by the lake and fed the fish as well. In the evening we went to a Vietnamese restaurant with Aroonsri and had a five hour discussion about various aspects of her work at MSU.

The journey to Chiang Mai went well. As we waited for our connection in the Don Muang domestic terminal we met both Aroonsri and Wittya on their way back to Khon Kaen after morning meetings in Bangkok. There was a little hitch in Chiang Mai when we collected our hold baggage. All three pieces of luggage had a viscous pinkish brown coloured liquid on them. When we were not able to remove the liquid very effectively with paper tissues we asked where we could lodge a complaint about the contamination. We were directed to the 'Lost and Found' office. The problem was pretty much beyond their expertise. Their advice was for us to check into our hotel and then completely empty our baggage and leave the empty baggage at the hotel reception. They would send someone round to clean them up! Apart from being inconvenient it was quite impracticable as there is never enough space in a hotel room to unpack big cases completely. Our chief concern was whether the liquid had entered the cases or not. In fact it had not and so I cleaned the outside of the cases and the plastic holdall myself.

We had been met and delivered to the Amari Rincome Hotel by a CMU Faculty of Pharmacy minibus. Shortly after entering our hotel room the phone rang and our friend Dr. Jaratbhan, the former Dean of the Faculty, welcomed us and invited us out for dinner at the Regent Resort Hotel. This is situated about 5 miles outside Chiang Mai in the countryside and is the place where Mrs. Clinton and such people have stayed.

We arrived at the entrance to the Regent Spa just before dark and walked towards the hotel reception area through the quite extensive grounds. This took us past quite large holiday houses built in a striking architectural style which was possibly predominantly Burmese. The Thai food was delicious and I would say it probably could not be bettered anywhere.

On Saturday morning I contacted the Thai Airways office in Chiang Mai by phone. I was given the good news that I now had a confirmed seat, together with Joan, on the 7.15 pm plane from Chiang Mai on 2 January, arriving Bangkok 8.25 pm, in good time to connect with the 11.25 pm KLM flight to Amsterdam. Praise the Lord, this was the breakthrough we needed.

In the evening I watched some English Premier

League football on our hotel TV. In Thailand there is good support for English football and Thai men are knowledgeable about players and clubs. As a result football can make a useful starter topic of conversation.

Boon collected us at 10.00 am to take us to the morning service at the First Thai Church which is about 130 years old. Unfortunately we arrived not long before the end of the service, which had begun at 9.30 am, so we decided to stay on for the next service at 11.30 am. However, at the end of the first service we did meet up with Woraporn and her husband.

Woraporn is a lecturer in the Faculty of Pharmacy and in conversation she mentioned that Phayap University, which is a private university founded by the Presbyterian Church, was planning to start a Health Sciences Faculty and they would like to include Pharmacy. We thought that we might hear more about this during our stay in Chiang Mai but nothing materialised.

In the afternoon we set off with Boon to find Andrew and Shona Goodman and family who were working as missionaries, among the Shan people, with the Overseas Missionary Fellowship in Maehongson. They were in Chiang Mai for the birth of their fourth child. Our church in Aberdeen supported Andrew and Shona and we wanted to see how they were and pass on greetings from our church. I had phoned Andrew on Saturday and was told that their baby boy, Isaac Peter, had been born on the previous Monday. Shona and Isaac were both doing well and they hoped to return to Maehongson on Monday 23 December. I asked if we might meet them at the First Thai Church on Sunday. Andrew said they went to another church which was called the Grace Church, but he did not say where that church was. We wrongly assumed it was near to where they were staying at the Mekong Centre. We agreed that we would visit them about 3.30 pm on Sunday and I was given directions of how to get there. It was quite hard to locate the Mekong Centre, but after asking three different people we found someone who pointed out a big building which could be seen over the rooftops and was only about 100 yards away. It was the Mekong Center and had only recently been completed. We had a good visit and were very pleased to see that Shona and Isaac looked well as there had been considerable concern towards the end of the pregnancy and Shona had been moved to Chiang Mai for treatment and to await the birth. This had provoked much prayer, including by their friends in Gilcomston. In the Lord's goodness all was well. After Andrew had shown us round the Mekong Centre and explained to us some of the things that were going on there we had a time of prayer and then took our leave.

On Monday we went to the Faculty of Pharmacy where Joan and I spoke briefly with Dean Aurawan and Associate Professor Porntip. We were told that the next day they planned to take us for a celebratory Chinese meal together with the senior members of the faculty.

On Monday afternoon I was introduced to Mrs. Siriphorn, a lecturer, who was studying for a PhD with Jaratbhan. I was asked to give her practice in English conversation. This I did while she drove me to the particularly Chinese section of Chiang Mai, by the Chang Moy Road, and showed me around the indoor market and pointed out to me the most popular food sellers. There were a lot of visitors from Bangkok, at that time, and they were crowding around certain stalls while ignoring others which were apparently displaying the same food speciality. On the way back again Siriphorn pointed out to me some interesting shops not far from our hotel and the house where the President of Chiang Mai University, Dr. Nipon, lived. Dr Nipon, a pharmacist, obtained his PhD from the University of Strathclyde, Glasgow.

In the evening we ate out with Porntip, her husband Khung, and their son and daughter. Both Porntip and Khung had undertaken postgraduate studies at the University of Bath and we found that we had quite a few things in common. I did the laboratory work for my London PhD at Bristol College of Science and Technology, which became the University of Bath very shortly after I left. One of the people I worked alongside, and was very friendly with, was George Fletcher who became a lecturer at the university and settled in Bath. During their time in Bath Porntip and Khung were invited to spend Christmas day with the Fletchers. Now Porntip, Khung, their daughter and son were taking us out to a meal at Christmas time. The food was very good and we had many interesting topics for discussion

Tuesday 24 December was a day when we experienced the Lord's blessing and leading in some striking ways. After breakfast we went for a walk down the road towards the Faculty. My intention was to point out to Joan some of the places Siriphorn had pointed out to me, including Dr. Nipon's house. We walked down the lane next to Nipon's house and turned left at a junction walking past a newly built house which was for sale or rent. Then we walked past a block of flats that was under construction and we came to a notice 'The Grace Church'. We stopped outside and out came Pastor Isara and Miss Watanavadee, a lecturer in statistics in the Faculty of Science. Pastor Isara had recently been the Pastor of Manorom church for six years and thus knew some people that we knew – even though we worked there 1959-1962. Watanavadee, or Dee for short, had become a Christian three years before through a man in Bangkok, who was the younger brother of Suwatt, who we knew very well. Then we were told that Dr Henry lived just round the corner. We also knew Henry from our Bangkok days, 1965-1969. Henry had been the first Principal of the now well respected Bangkok Bible College and after his retirement from working with OMF had returned to Thailand to work in Chiang Mai. We were a little disappointed to learn that the Grace Church had celebrated Christmas the previous Sunday and that they would not be having any special services on Christmas Eve or Christmas day. This was possibly an influence that had originated from overseas churches. It made us think of when we first arrived in Thailand when we were spending six weeks at Lopburi with Grace and Em Fry from America. This time with Em and Grace was in order to have some language study before we went to the Manorom Christian Hospital to work as pharmacists. Easter occurred while we were at Lopburi and we were surprised to find that we were scheduled for a full day of language study on Good Friday.

Just after returning to our hotel room we received a phone call from Dr. Thararat (nicknamed Fon), who we find is a very encouraging Christian and who is currently a lecturer in Food Science at Mae Jo University, about 15 miles outside Chiang Mai. Thararat visited us in Aberdeen several times during the time she was working on her PhD at Strathclyde University. She had returned to Thailand while we were working in Mahasrakham and had unsuccessfully tried to contact us. While chatting with Porntip the previous evening we had mentioned Thararat in connection with food science, because Porntip's daughter was studying food science at Chiang Mai. Tuesday morning Porntip had managed to contact Thararat and gave her our phone number. We were thrilled to re-establish contact and arranged to meet at Mae Jo University on Boxing Day.

Our celebratory lunch was held at the Chiang Mai Orchid Hotel and we were almost overwhelmed with kindness by the Dean and her team of senior academics. I was presented with a large silver plate which was suitably inscribed.

Joan was given a silver bowl standing on a silver plate. In the bowl was a plant oasis into which had been arranged the stems of a bunch of lovely pink roses. The plate was inscribed as follows:

'Chiang Mai University Faculty of Pharmacy Presented to Mrs. Joan Richards for her outstanding support to Professor RME Richards December 24, 2002.'

We were very impressed with their thoughtfulness and it meant a lot to both of us.

During the meal the Dean of the Faculty asked me why we had gone to Rhodesia to start a Pharmacy Degree there. I replied that we sought to go were God was leading us and we believed that He would have us go to Rhodesia at that time (1973-1978) and so we went.

In the evening Porntip had arranged for a faculty driver to collect us at 7.00pm and take us together with her son Laa and his friend Jack to the Candlelight Service at the First Thai Church. Both lads had been students at the Prince Royal Christian School which was founded by the Presbyterian missionaries in the middle 1800s when Chiang Mai was still independent from Thailand. Laa was studying third year medicine and Jack was studying third year pharmacy. Both had good English but Jack was quite shy. Joan did most of her speaking to Jack and I to Laa.

We arrived at the church with time to spare so after collecting our candles we sat down in one of the pews together. The church was beautifully decorated with flowers and an abundance of poinsettia plants in pots. Poinsettia trees are regarded to be Christmas trees by some people in Thailand. The red and green of the poinsettia was taken up with the red and green cloth draped across the back wall of the church and around pieces of church furniture. There were many candle stands with candles of different sizes. Our personal candles, with their little cardboard shields below the wick to protect the hand from hot candle fat, were the smallest. We had programmes in Thai which we started to look through. I used my programme to explain in more detail the Gospel message to Laa. When we were well through the programme it suddenly dawned on Laa that I was reading and expanding on what was written in Thai. 'Can you read Thai then?' he asked in amazement. Later in the service a girl of about seven years old sitting in the pew in front of us sat gazing at me in amazement that I was singing in Thai. Most foreigners who turned up at this church in Chiang Mai were short term visitors or business people who have not had the opportunity to learn Thai and are dependent on someone who can speak English explaining to them what is happening.

The candle light service was a very good service and the minister based his message on Philippians chapter two 'let this attitude be in you that was in Christ.' After the service finished at around 9.30 pm the congregation was invited to light their candles again and walk across the Nawarat Bridge to the Governor of Chiang Mai's house on the other bank of the River Ping. Several hundred went and we stood in the Governor's garden and sang carols. When the recently appointed Governor, his wife and some officials came out one of the ministers of the church gave him a brief history of the church and a summary of the Christmas message. He also told him that we had come to sing carols and to pray for him and his administration. Then the minister prayed at considerable length and in considerable detail for the Governor's administration and for the citizens of Chiang Mai city and province. The Governor, who was new to his position, then made a speech in reply and invited us to help ourselves to refreshments that he had prepared for us and which were laid out on tables in his garden. At this stage we felt it was time to leave and Laa phoned for the driver to come and collect us at the front of the church. By the time we had walked back over the bridge the driver was just arriving, so it all worked out very well and we had enjoyed a wonderful day.

On Christmas day our Bible reading contained the following verse 'From the fullness of His Grace we have all received one blessing after another.' (John chapter 1 verse 16) That had certainly been our experience during this visit to Thailand.

On the evening of Christmas day we went to a communal meal at the First Thai Church followed by a carol service and gospel presentation. This was primarily intended for disabled and disadvantaged people. We were very interested to see this involvement of the church with some of Chiang Mai's more vulnerable people.

Porntip had arranged for a faculty van to pick us up at 2.00 pm on Boxing Day and she accompanied us out to Mae Jo to see Thararat and her Christian Russian husband Alex. We had not met Alex before and it was at least three years since we had seen

Thararat. Members of the Chemistry and the Biology Departments had heard we were visiting and they wanted to show us round their laboratories and tell us something about the research they were doing. This was very interesting and took the first hour or so. Then we went to Thararat's house where Alex was waiting for us. Alex had studied law in Russia and after studying one year of theology at St.Andrew's University he studied for his PhD in law at Glasgow University. There he met Thararat. In Thailand he teaches law at CMU and English conversation at Mae Jo University. When we met him he was in the process of making the mixture to prepare pancakes. This he did quite deliberately and methodically for some time after we arrived while giving us a discourse on the history, geographical spread and cultural implications of the pancake. After some encouragement from his wife he started to cook his first pancake. By this time a wide range of accompanying spreads had been assembled, the prize one of which was honey produced by Alex's relatives living in the forests of Siberia. This was such a precious and rare commodity that one had to ask oneself which would be the better course of action to take. To decline Alex's precious commodity on the basis that it meant so much to him that it would be cruel to unnecessarily diminish his irreplaceable supply? Or, on the other hand, after hearing the virtues of such a unique product extolled would it be callous and rude to decline to eat it? Those who know me would guess that I would err on the side of enjoying his honey with him before some unknown disaster might take it away from both of us! I ended up having two of his large pancakes – both with Siberian honey. Again it was a time of very profitable conversations in addition to our learning more about the wonder of the pancake. While I was talking to Alex at one end of the table the others were having their own conversation at the other end of the table, included in which was Thararat's response to Porntip's question, 'How did you become a Christian?' Thararat asked me to pray before we left and reluctantly bade our farewells.

There was a party at the Faculty for staff and students on Friday, even though some students still had classes and even examinations over the weekend. We had learned that the basic requirements at these parties were to join in were possible and enjoy those parts that could be enjoyed. When Dr. Watcharee's request for student volunteers to sing 'We wish you a Happy Christmas' in English with her met no response I saw it as an opportunity to help with something that was easy to do. Joan and Aurawan also joined in. Later on we also took part in one traditional circle dance (ramwong).

A student, Ann, from Paknampho in the north part of Central Thailand, came and had a little chat with me in English which I thought was very bold and friendly of her. She said that she would not be going home for New Year because all the trains were full and she could not get a ticket. Where had I heard that before?

On Saturday another lecturer, Pariya, spent the day with us. We have known Pariya for about ten years and at one stage she took a three month course at RGU. The original plan was that Boon would drive us to the Queen's botanical garden in the morning but first Boon had to collect two people from the morning train from Bangkok. This train was five hours behind schedule so we had a change of plan and switched the botanical garden visit to the afternoon. In the morning Pariya first took us to an exhibition of mostly flowers, vegetables and fruit that had been produced through a Royal Project. This display was open to the public for just a few days. Then we visited the Chiang Mai museum which Pariya had not visited before. We found it very interesting, especially when we came to the section which dealt with the recent history of Chiang Mai. We were surprised to learn that Chiang Mai only officially became a part of Thailand in 1933 after the railway line was constructed. Another interesting piece of information was that David Richardson, a British explorer and diplomat seems to have been the first westerner to come to Chiang Mai in the 1820s. Trade between Chiang Mai and western countries gradually developed after that time but it was by way of Burma and not Thailand. There are many other interesting things we hope to be able to learn from visiting the Museum at a future date.

Some glass houses had been built since our last visit to the Queen's Botanical Gardens. The tropical rain forest building was said to be the largest glass house in SE Asia. Most of the flowering plants were in a dormant period because it was the cool season. Nevertheless the trees, shrubs and grass were all in good order and looked well cared for. In the evening we ate at an open air restaurant, on agricultural ministry land, on the side of a small hill overlooking Chiang Mai and to one side of the university. A few hundred other people had the same idea and it was obviously a place that had pleasant memories for many of the University Alumni who were holidaying in Chiang Mai.

On Sunday morning we walked to the Grace Church arriving about 10.20 am. Standing at the entrance to the church was a somewhat worried looking Boet Stoffberg, an ex OMF missionary from South Africa. We had been good friends with Boet when we lived in Bangkok and he worked with young people in South Thailand. Later we met him again several times when we were living in Salisbury, Rhodesia and he was on home assignment in Cape Town. Boet was worried because he had lost contact with a Thai friend on Saturday evening and he had thought that he would see him at church. When he wasn't there Boet concluded that he may have been involved in some accident, or he had got lost. The friend turned up about five minutes after us and Boet became more like his normal self. We were very pleased to have renewed contact with Boet and to learn that he was still involved in Christian work in Thailand. Inside the church a Bible study was in progress which was being led by Henry Briedenthal. We were made to feel very much at home among those attending the morning service, who mainly consisted of students and young people, but with a sprinkling of university lecturers, OMFers and other

Christian workers. At lunchtime we spoke with Sam Wunderli, an OMF missionary from Switzerland, and learnt some more of the work of the Mekong Centre.

In the late afternoon we went to the Chiang Mai Community Church, which meets at The First Thai Church premises 5.00-6.30 pm. This church is for the international community of Chiang Mai and visitors to the city. We were very pleased to meet up with Dr. Chris Maddox, who was the Medical Superintendent at Manorom Christian Hospital when we worked there. He has lived in Chiang Mai for many years and is now in his nineties, but still able to drive himself to church! We also met Molly Clive, another former colleague from Manorom, Andy Thompson was just passing through returning from India, where he has children at Hebron school, to East Malaysia where he teaches in a Bible College. Andy was originally from Rhodesia and his OMF application was processed when I was on the OMF South African Council. At one time he and his wife worked in Chiang Mai. Over the years our paths have crossed on several occasions. Another person who came to speak to us was the missionary with the American Nazarene Church who we had last seen when he had accompanied the group of Americans on their visit to Mahasarakham to help with the church building. It can be seen that Chiang Mai is quite an important centre for Christian work and activity.

On this latest visit to NE Thailand and Chiang Mai we had the privilege of worshipping with several different Christian church groups and meeting many helpful and encouraging individuals, both

Christian and others. We felt very encouraged that again prayer had been answered. A glance at the prayer items mentioned in the first paragraph of this chapter will confirm that this was so.

Monday was taken as a day of preparation for our travel home on Tuesday evening. The overnight flight went well and, although we arrived back to snow, we had a warm house waiting that Tom had prepared for us. We had experienced almost a month of wonderful Thai hospitality and the 'Mahasarakham Prescription' itemised in the first chapter, although at times seemingly impossible to dispense, had with the Lord's enabling not only been dispensed but had produced a product that left a nice taste in our mouths. We are also very encouraged with the continued outworking, under God's good hand, of the product of the 'Test Prescription', to the blessing of many churches and individuals. Would there be further assignments? That was in the Lord's hands.

Printed in the United Kingdom
by Lightning Source UK Ltd.
120489UK00001B/42